Pluralist Publics in Market-Driven Education

Also available from Bloomsbury

Evidence-Informed Policy and Practice in Education, Chris Brown
Higher Education and the Public Good: Imagining the University, Jon Nixon
Why Universities Should Seek Happiness and Contentment, Paul Gibbs

Pluralist Publics in Market-Driven Education

Towards More Democracy in Educational Reform

Ruth Boyask

BLOOMSBURY ACADEMIC
LONDON • NEW YORK • OXFORD • NEW DELHI • SYDNEY

BLOOMSBURY ACADEMIC
Bloomsbury Publishing Plc
50 Bedford Square, London, WC1B 3DP, UK
1385 Broadway, New York, NY 10018, USA

BLOOMSBURY, BLOOMSBURY ACADEMIC and the Diana logo are trademarks of
Bloomsbury Publishing Plc

First published in Great Britain 2020

Copyright © Ruth Boyask, 2020

Ruth Boyask has asserted her right under the Copyright, Designs and Patents Act, 1988,
to be identified as Author of this work.

For legal purposes the Acknowledgements on p. x–xi constitute an extension
of this copyright page.

Cover design: Tjasa Krivec
Cover image: Interesting People who Care (2019) (© photo by Dale Johnson)

All rights reserved. No part of this publication may be reproduced or transmitted
in any form or by any means, electronic or mechanical, including photocopying,
recording, or any information storage or retrieval system, without prior
permission in writing from the publishers.

Bloomsbury Publishing Plc does not have any control over, or responsibility for, any
third-party websites referred to or in this book. All internet addresses given in this
book were correct at the time of going to press. The author and publisher regret any
inconvenience caused if addresses have changed or sites have ceased to exist,
but can accept no responsibility for any such changes.

A catalogue record for this book is available from the British Library.

A catalog record for this book is available from the Library of Congress.

ISBN: HB: 978-1-3500-5450-9
ePDF: 978-1-3500-5451-6
eBook: 978-1-3500-5452-3

Typeset by Newgen KnowledgeWorks Pvt. Ltd., Chennai, India

To find out more about our authors and books visit www.bloomsbury.com and
sign up for our newsletters.

To Darren, Lily and Doris

Contents

List of Tables	ix
Acknowledgements	x
Introduction	1

1   Visualizing Pluralist Public Education   5
    Public education   5
    A methodology for policy as practice   9
    The structure of the book   16

2   Theorizing Pluralist Public Education   23
    Publics and their opinion   27
    The greater community of the twenty-first century   32
    Who is the public in public schooling?   34
    The uncommon public school   37
    Conclusion   41

3   Opening a Window on the Private Sphere   43
    Private education   46
    Limits to public purposes of private schools   50
    Conditional publicness in English private schools   53
    Privatized education   56
    Privatization in schooling   61

4   Mapping Governance Structures   65
    Struggle for the public in conditional public entities   68
    Corporations: For the benefit of members?   72
    Charitable, not-for-profit and public benefit organizations   75
    Public–private partnerships   78
    The rise of social enterprise and for-profit public benefit   80
    Mapping structural forms   82

5	Public Benefit/Public Good	85
	Contested purposes of schooling	90
	Governance for the public good in private sector schooling	92
	Conditional equality in private schooling: A research study	96
	Governance in the case study schools	100
	The extent and nature of the public good	105
6	Pluralist Public Accountability	109
	The school	115
	The research project	118
	Classification and framing within the projects	119
	Participation and learning inside the projects	122
	Democratic participation in education markets	126
	Public accountability in a conditional counterpublic	129
7	Bounded Public Service	133
	Relations between local authorities and schools	137
	Models of service	138
	Corporate model	139
	Community engagement model	140
	Entrepreneurial model	141
	Co-operative model	143
	Implications of reform across the local government sector	144
	Discussion	146
8	Public Education Unbounded	149
	Recontextualization in the academies programme	151
	Policy to support democratic publics	154
	Closing thoughts	159
References		161
Index		175

Tables

5.1	The eighteen case study schools	101
6.1	Evidence of learning and the nature of participation	125
7.1	Case studies: The local authorities	137
7.2	Models of service: Local authorities	138

Acknowledgements

This book has been formed by twenty years of thought, writing and research. In that time many people have contributed to my work or shaped my thinking and deserve thanks.

I would especially like to thank the students and staff I met at the schools where I have researched. Some of the schools are identified by name in the book because their special character was so rare it was impossible and not desirable to obscure. All the schools I have studied deserve admiration and recognition in their efforts towards democracy even if the prevailing conditions have not readily supported them.

Thanks are due to Jean C. McPhail, Kathleen Quinlivan and Baljit Kaur for prompting me originally to think about public education differently.

The research reported in Chapter 5 was supported by a British Academy/Leverhulme grant. Jennifer Lea and Alison Black both made substantial and valued contributions to the data collection for this project.

The research reported in Chapter 7 was supported by a small grant from the British Educational Leadership, Management and Administration Society (BELMAS) as part of their Structural Reform Research Programme. I would especially like to thank Tim Simkins and Philip Woods for convening this programme of research and our seminar meetings where I learnt a great deal more about the policy context of English schools. Thanks are due also to Howard Stevenson, Helen Gunter and Pat Thomson for convening the BELMAS Critical Educational Policy and Leadership Studies research interest group whose discussions on public education were vitally important to the development of this book.

The empirical research in Chapters 5 and 7 has been previously reported in the following publications and republished here in accordance with Sage Journals permissions policy:

Boyask, R. (2015). 'Nuanced Understandings of Privatization in Local Authorities' Services to Schools'. *Management in Education*, 29(1): 35–40.

Boyask, R. (2015). 'The Public Good in English Private School Governance'. *European Educational Research Journal*, 14(6): 566–81.

Acknowledgements

Thanks are due to the publishers at Symposium Books Ltd for the permission to reproduce in Chapter 2 portions of copyright material from the following work:

Boyask, R. (2019). 'Educating Publics in the Greater Community'. *FORUM*, 61(3): 307–17. http://doi.org/10.15730/forum.2019.61.3.307.

Introduction

Sands School is a privately funded secondary school situated in the main street of a prosperous, ancient market town in the south-west of England. The school premises are a charming, large, but slightly ramshackle, period town house with gardens that do justice to a Romantic poet's imagination. While there are over two thousand privately funded schools in England, this one is especially notable for its special democratic character. As a private school it is exempt from oversight by a democratically elected public authority, yet its curriculum, pedagogy and governance are founded on principles of democratic equality. At Sands School, students and teachers alike are actively engaged in debate, reflection and decision-making on issues that affect them. It is one of a handful of schools in England that run on explicitly democratic principles, like the nearby primary Park School in Dartington, and the better-known Summerhill School in Suffolk that was established in 1921 by progressive educator A. S. Neill. These schools are democratic inasmuch as they promote equality, freedom and participation in governance for their citizenry, yet their status as fee-charging schools means that citizenship rights are usually conditional on students' capacity to pay. Does restricted access cancel out schools' commitment to democracy and associated principles of equality and social justice? Or is there something salvageable in the conditional equality they offer that can help us in the construction of a fairer and more equal world? This book is written on the presumption that there is something of value to be learnt from such individual schools. It presumes that careful examination of tensions within such sites and other educational settings and the ways that such concerns are negotiated through easy or uneasy compromise can help us to understand and perhaps address these tensions when they occur elsewhere. Similar tensions are reproduced on national and even transnational scales; and so, the purpose of this book is to extend outwards through robust analytical methods and frameworks our understanding of the tensions and compromises found within specific educational sites, towards further understanding of public education, its policy and systems.

Elsewhere schools like the private democratic schools in England are regarded as alternative schools because they are set apart from mainstream schooling by their educational philosophy (Carnie, 2003; Kraftl, 2014), and this tends to be how they describe themselves. This book, however, is not about alternative education; it is about public education and the centrality of education to democratic society. Democratic schools like Sands are not benign alternatives to mainstream schooling where ideal forms of democracy and equality flourish. They are more than philosophically different from the majority of schools. Their location in the private school sector sets them apart from mainstream state-funded schooling and makes them materially different; their restricted access aligns them with other private schools that are bastions of middle-class virtue and contributors to social disadvantage and segregation. Indeed, democratic private schooling seems antithetical to traditional views of public education because of its restricted access. Horace Mann's (1837–1848) foundational reports on public schooling in the United States described principles underlying a common or public school as a 'free district school, sufficiently safe, and sufficiently good, *for all the children within its territory*' (Mann, 1957, p. 32, emphasis added). Mann extends the principle of equality of access to advanced schooling, claiming that sharing a common or communal education will foster familiarity and 'fraternal feelings' within local communities. A fundamental platform for democratic education according to Fielding and Moss (2010) in their comparatively recent reconceptualization of schooling along democratic lines is the democratic common school that similarly is at its most basic level open to all who live within its locality. So, what, if anything, do private democratic schools such as Sands with their restricted access and private funding have to do with public education?

In this book you will read case studies of different educational institutions and organizations, including Sands. To a greater or lesser extent these educational settings are private in the sense that they are set apart from the mainstream and consequently removed from aspects of state governmental control. In some cases, the origins of their private statuses are defined because their forms are historical and predate the social institutions of a modern democratic state. In others they are the outcomes of modern processes of privatization or a withdrawal from the public sphere as it is variously defined (Starr, 1988). However, it is their public rather than private status that is the focus of this book. In order to understand how these entities can be conceptualized as public or why it may be important to do so requires me to set out some foundations for this argument. First, it requires conceptually disentangling the public from the state, and public education from state-funded education, while retaining recognition of their interrelationships.

1

Visualizing Pluralist Public Education

Public education

The most heavy-handed and polemical distinctions equate the public with the state and private with the market (Starr, 1988). While this distinction seems to be common sense in a market-driven education system, it excludes multiple interests from both domains and glosses over the complexity of relations between the state and market, and relations between the public and both state and market. According to education policy scholars Robertson et al. (2012), the distinction comes from the field of economics, whereas critical education policy studies favours a culturalist view that considers the concepts of public and private to be socially and culturally contested and defined. If you examine critically from a culturalist perspective the assumptions that the public nature of public education is its association with the state sector and that the private nature of private education is its association with the market, there are evident holes. Education, even at its most market-like, is not founded on purely market principles, and in the state's withdrawal from the public through privatization or in its relegation of education to private entities there is never complete withdrawal. The state regulates privatized and private sector institutions and organizations, for example, through corporate, equalities or even education law. Indeed, in England both private and privatized (academy) schools are classified as independent schools, subject to the Education (Independent School Standards) Regulations 2014. Regulation in both private sector and privatized institutions is an enactment of governmental responsibility for the public good. Government retains the responsibility for upholding some form of public good even when it commissions private entities to fulfil its obligations, even though what is meant by the public good depends upon the definition of the public and how its interests are defined (see Chapter 5 for a detailed exploration of the contested nature of the public good). Recognizing the public as irreducible to the state is important to understanding the public good of public education and why we need to problematize associating public education solely with the public sector of the state. While an ideal democratic state is, by its nature, responsible for upholding the public good, actually existing national democracies are far from ideal. In defining public education this book presumes the following in respect of the state. First, that the state does not always fulfil its public responsibilities, whether through misrecognition of the public and its interests or through neglect. Second, that government regulation in the public interest may, and often does, go awry. Third, governmental power that works towards the public good is not necessarily transparent or embodied in government agents. Fourth, the enactment of the public good through education is not a straightforward matter of transfer from policy into practice.

If public education is associated with the state sector, as is commonly understood, then the privatization of government responsibilities and assets and multiplying public–private partnerships means it is hard to distinguish between public and private entities. While complex relations between the state, individuals and organizations outside of the state have long existed, much recent education policy work shows an intense and extensive expansion of private interests into all aspects of public qua state policy following earlier curriculum, assessment and educational administrative reforms of the United States, United Kingdom and New Zealand in the 1980s (Ball and Youdell, 2008; Wylie, 2009). This book illustrates what remains of the public interest in government education policy and practice transformed by neoliberal ideologies and the use of market mechanisms to address social need. Yet the most important contribution the book makes is to show that this policy context confuses and confounds common-sense understandings of public education. Reducing the public in public education to a location in the state sector is not helpful when the state sector has eminently permeable boundaries and the state acts, at least in significant part, in the interests of elite individuals and the corporations that support them. To further public education as both ideal and practice, we need a much more nuanced understanding of what is in the public interest, how the public is constituted and how we might define public education. And so the aims of this book are to set out some of the arguments that problematize common-sense concepts of public education, show some ways forward for its future development and make apparent that the reconceptualization of public education is an ongoing project.

I have used the example of Sands, a school understood as a private school in its conventional sense, deliberately in the introduction of this book about public education to unsettle any taken-for-granted assumptions about what counts. Sands demonstrates that those committed to furthering the public interest through education may make use of whatever means are at hand, including entities that share ownership with private actors or even entities that are situated within what we commonly refer to as the private education sector. However, to understand the relationship between Sands and public education beyond the school's democratic good intentions, you need a more refined understanding of what counts as public. Clarifying what we mean when we talk about the public in terms such as public education or the public good shows that public spaces can be found in unlikely places.

The public in the book's title and the public education enacted in its interest are therefore a qualified or conditional type, where the public aspect of educational policy and practice has degrees of 'publicness'. The term 'publicness' used here describes the changing qualities of being public, that is, the 'fluid, dynamic and elusive character of publicness' (Newman, 2007, p. 888) that becomes lost in the reification evident in terms such as 'the public', 'the public sphere' or 'the public good'. The conditional publicness of public entities, which is partial and contextually defined within educational sites like Sands, is put under scrutiny in this book. The examined educational sites are not public in the way that public education is defined in the everyday world, that is, regarded as education funded by the state (although some of the other examples of education included in the book are state-funded institutions). They must also not be confused with the term 'public schooling' that is reserved for England's most elite private schools, which originally had a connection to the concept of the public because many of them were originally established to educate a broader section of society, but in recent times provide high fee-paying education almost exclusively to the wealthiest (Kynaston and Green, 2019). As shown earlier they are not even public in Mann's sense of common and free to all. Public education as it is conceptualized here is connected to the deeper tradition that links people with democratic participation but extends this notion in the light of contemporary theorizations of the public sphere. Public education is not located within a single, unified public space defined in terms of its funding basis (i.e. dividing public from private sector) or a proxy for talking about schools solely as an apparatus for exercising state control, either of which may work against the public interest. Instead it follows Nancy Fraser (1990) by conceiving the public as multiple, so that public education is defined by difference and variation in respect of its constituents and their opinions, and educational organizations are governed by multiple educational publics that inhabit multiple public spheres.[1]

Public sphere theory helps to conceptualize the public sphere not as a single site but as multiple sites where groups of people who legitimately carry the public opinion of their group (Fraser, 1990; Habermas, 1991), or publics, participate in governance through democratic processes of opinion-formation and decision-making. While the public sphere in European political thought has an intimate connection with the nation state, Fraser's (1990; 2014) reconceptualization of the public sphere extends the notion to other institutions that exert governmental control. In this she follows other social scientists who conceptualize social coordination as governance, which is a broader concept than government because it recognizes that regulatory practices are exercised through different forms of organization (Bevir, 2012). The broadening of the public sphere is an important departure when recognizing that some groups are excluded from or marginalized within the mainstream public sphere associated with the state, and potentially allows disenfranchised groups to construct for themselves new, legitimate authority through what Fraser terms 'subaltern' or 'counterpublics'. It also brings into consideration publics that are larger than national polities, potentially providing a counterbalance to conceptualizing transnational education policy reform solely as the preserve of private networks of influence. Institutions governed outside of the direct control of the nation state tend to be classed as private in its terms, which removes them from its public sphere and sets them outside of its public scrutiny. Analyses of schools like Sands help us to work our way through these problems by showing how publicness can manifest in different forms and, when such schools are examined in relation to more conventional forms of public education, contribute to an overall and more refined picture of public education and accountability.

Hence what is explored in this book is the nature of the public and its qualities of publicness in educational sites like the private democratic schools, the make-up of their educational publics and the extent to which they engage their publics in democratic processes. In this book privately funded educational spaces are not set apart from public education but are examined alongside educational sites that are closer to common-sense and reified understandings of public education. These sites also exhibit tensions between possibilities for and restrictions upon freedom, equality and justice. Included in the educational sites are also examples of local government services to schools that are either partially or fully privatized as a result of changes to funding arrangements, and new state-funded semi-autonomous schools such as Tomorrow's schools in New Zealand, charter schools in the United States, free schools in Sweden, independent public schools in Australia and academy schools in England. The appearance of new models of schools that are funded by the state and privately governed is a transnational phenomenon (Brewer and Hentschke, 2009), recognized and commended in reports from the Organisation for Economic Co-operation and Development's (OECD) PISA comparative study of national education systems (OECD, 2012). 'In general, privately managed schools tend to have more autonomy, better resources, better school climate and better performance levels than publicly managed schools' (OECD, 2012, p. 18). The OECD defines such schools as 'private' because while they are funded by the public purse, they are privately governed and managed, and exercise control over their own resources. Such schools typify the deliberate blurring of lines between public and private in the national policies of countries influenced by economic globalization and neoliberal theories of public choice and human capital (Lubienski, 2001; Olssen and Peters, 2005). The purpose of examining publicness in examples of private education is not to further blur these lines but rather to feature an analytical framework that conceptually distinguishes between public, state and market. While there are evident overlaps between state and public sphere, and private and market, a robust analysis recognizes clear differences between these categories so that their functions are not subsumed. It is important to differentiate state from public when the state acts outside of the public interest through exclusion or marginalization of individuals and groups. At a time when essential social functions are ever more outsourced from the state through privatization it is also important to retain public scrutiny and influence over the organizations that perform these functions regardless of their economic status. Reclaiming them as public education holds them to account for the public good.

A methodology for policy as practice

In Christchurch, New Zealand, in 2001 a new publicly funded primary school opened above a city pub. In 2002 it shifted to a purpose-designed and -built premises on the top floors of an inner-city building. I was part of a research team, led by Dr Jean McPhail, who documented its opening in the new premises and embarked upon an ethnographic, longitudinal study to examine the quality of learning in a school that unlike other state-funded schools defined itself through its orientation to learning within its founding documents. At the official opening New Zealand's then minister of education, Honourable Trevor Mallard, stated that 'to be honest, Discovery 1 is very much on the edge of my personal comfort zone as far as education is concerned' (Boyask et al., 2008). Discovery

1 school differed from other new schools because it made use of neoliberal educational administration reforms of the Education Act 1989 that allowed for independently governed schools (as all New Zealand schools had become through the Tomorrow's Schools policy) to adopt the status of a Designated Character School, which was a designation usually reserved for schools whose special character was immersive Māori language teaching. The special character of Discovery 1 was its philosophy of discovery learning that was articulated in its mission statement as 'Free to discover, to uncover, create your own path!' Students were admitted to the school by a selection policy that looked for commitment by parents and children to this philosophy. Discovery learning was intended to be enacted through the negotiation of individual learning plans within an equal partnership between learning adviser (which was the new title given to the school's teachers), parent and child. While learning advisers, parents, children and school founders shared optimism for the benefits of Discovery learning, the research project revealed tensions that emerged in enactment of the philosophy. In practice, the anticipated freedoms were curtailed, as traditional practices of schooling such as rote learning and behaviour management that proved to be deep-seated habits of mind for teachers and parents alike competed and sometimes meshed with the innovations brought into the school from 'the everyday values and practices of the business world' (McPhail and Palincsar, 2009, p. 139).

Ethnographic work undertaken during its first three years of operation revealed Discovery 1 struggled to enact freedom and innovation through its policy of equality in learning. Throughout this period there were also struggles around governance, with community meetings that sought to build consensus through discussion, development of communal agreements and establishment of a teacher–parent research community. Despite these early experiments with democratic governance within the school community, by 2006 the Education Review Office, the New Zealand schools' inspection agency, was reporting a history of conflict and contestation in school governance and management that affected all the operations of the school. 'In the short history of the school the board, staff and parents have experienced some difficult periods that have resulted in turnover of staff, students and trustees' (Education Review Office, 2006). A supplementary review in 2007 indicated progress had been made in resolving these problems. Such conflicts might have been mitigated earlier with a clearer understanding of the different influences upon schooling, and a more realistic appreciation by school leaders and governors of how power operates to skew relationships even when they are intended to be equal. The actors within the microcosm of a school are oftentimes not well equipped to make sense of the wider social and political forces that shape their daily lives. It is good to know that the external review process by the government's inspectorate in this case led to greater stability in relations between governors and school, even though it provides little insight into how they were negotiating the different discourses the research found operating within the school and the ideological positions the overall governance of the school adopted in relation to competing discourses.

For the researchers Discovery 1 provided a window on the tensions at play in state policy between market forces and public interest. To understand how both the market and the public interest operate in this context you need a complex understanding of policy, the ways it discursively shapes thought and action, yet is a text open to reformulation through processes of translation and recontextualization (Ball, 2006). In the social sciences generally, there has been a move away from cause–effect models of social phenomena, such as policy, towards non-linear models and models of complexity (Sanderson, 2009). The way we think about policy analysis in educational research is much shaped by policy sociologists such as Jenny Ozga, Roger Dale and Stephen Ball. These researchers tend to work within a critical studies tradition, using critical, post-structural or post-humanist conceptual frameworks. Policy sociology is a term that comes from Ozga (1987), meaning policy study 'rooted in the social science tradition, historically informed and drawing on qualitative and illuminative techniques'. In his work on policy Ball has shifted understanding of policy so it is understood as more than a policy text that goes through a linear process from conceptualization through development to implementation, and instead acknowledges the complexity of the 'realpolitik of policy work' (Lingard and Sellar, 2013, p. 268).

The significance of policy as a form of social practice that is embedded within different social and cultural contexts is illustrated through Ball and Bowe's (1992) conceptualization of policy in the policy cycle. This is a model of policy that is based in the assumption that meanings of policy are shaped and formed within policy contexts through open-ended policy processes such as interpretation and translation. Policy is defined through a lens that has three different facets that are each contextually bound. The first facet of policy is intended policy, which highlights for policy researchers the context where official ideologies circulate, and authoritative policy decisions are made. Actual policy is a facet of policy that highlights 'the words' of policy legislation, documents and guidance, which is both intended policy that sets out to frame policy-in-use but is also open text that can be worked upon through the practice of policy through its ambiguities and silences. Policy-in-use is the practice of policy through its enactment and the discourses that emerge as policy actors engage with intended and actual policy. Policy-in-use is an especially useful concept for this book, which focuses upon the contexts of practice and their enactment of intended and actual policy. This multi-faceted framework for understanding policy is underpinned by Ball's (1993) dual ontology: policy as discourse and policy as text. Discourse in this sense is regulated practice, that is, following the philosopher Michel Foucault 'the rules and structures which produce particular utterances and texts' (Mills, 2004, p. 6), that is, policy as discourse is concerned with rules and how they act to govern rather than policy statements in a linguistic sense; however, policy as text refers to the encoded representations of meaning within intended and actual policy, including encoding through language and other forms of representation. Discursive and textual analyses come from different conceptual traditions, and their inclusion within a single analytical framework represents Ball's commitment to multi-theory explanations for the complexities evident in policy. He advocates for policy analysis that draws from a toolbox of different theoretical tools in recognition that education policy analysis is an applied field where ideals are only useful inasmuch as they illuminate practice. This position is consistent with approaching educational research from a pragmatic perspective and seeking to know the world and experience it through a variety of social science approaches (Biesta and Burbules, 2003). The investigations of social phenomena presented in the following chapters are underpinned by a pragmatist stance using the methodological tools most appropriate to the phenomenon under study. The studies examined throughout the book have adopted different research designs and utilize different methods, but they are all concerned with examining regulated practices in situ. The conceptualization of policy used is related to Ball's (2006) dual ontology of policy, as well as its extension by Singh, Thomas and Harris (2013) through the work of Basil Bernstein (2000) who defined a principle of recontextualization that operates within two fields: an official recontextualizing field (ORF) where state control dominates social action, and a pedagogic recontextualizing field (PRF) where social discourses are interpreted into pedagogic discourse. Within the ORF policy is enacted through an overt transference or diffusion of power through its encoded representations within policy artefacts or text. In the PRF the codes of policy are more subtly conveyed through processes of translation and learning, leaving open possibilities for miseducational or resistant interpretations of policy. It is important to note that Bernstein's concept of pedagogic discourse extends far beyond what we tend to think of as education, as the 'voice of pedagogic discourse is the dominant device of social control and identity formation during these times' (Singh, 2014, p. 8) within what Bernstein called the totally pedagogized society. Thus, all policy might be thought of as educational.

All relations that underpin recontextualization are relationships of power and control. Through processes of decoding and recoding policy, power is exercised, and control constrains possible action. Yet recontextualization of policy is a generative process with potential for opening regulatory, constraining and unjust policy discourses. Singh, Thomas and Harris (2013) highlight the role of policy intermediaries acting at levels between policy makers and policy enactors (teachers in their study), who influence the enactment of policy through their interpretations and translations. While differing interpretations of official discourse may exist in the ORF it is made up of agents whose role it is to represent dominant views of the state and therefore relatively homogeneous in its interpretation of policy. There is more likely diversity of ideals, knowledge and interpretations among agents operating in the PRF. Hence the state struggles for control over pedagogic discourse.

> If the PRF can have an effect on pedagogic discourse independently of the ORF, then there is both some autonomy and struggle over pedagogic discourse and its practices. But if there is only the ORF, then there is no autonomy. Today, the state is attempting to weaken the PRF through its ORF, and thus attempting to reduce relative autonomy over the construction of pedagogic discourse and over its social contexts. (Bernstein, 2000, p. 58)

Bernsteinian processes of framing through pedagogic discourse are examined in some detail in Chapter 6 within the context of curriculum reform at Sands School to show how dominant state discourses related to hierarchical and market forms of governance frame action within the school, even while it strives towards democratic practice; while this was not a conceptual tool used in understanding the forces at work within Discovery 1 similarities between the tensions observed there and those within the context of Sands suggest it could be useful. Bernstein's work is invaluable for understanding sociological issues embedded within the micro-settings of schools. His notion of pedagogic discourse provides an analytic framework for researching within educational settings that includes the nature of knowledge transmitted, how it is transmitted and whose knowledge is considered legitimate (Morais, 2002). At the time of the research Sands was a well-established school, and even though it had a developed philosophy of education, democracy still struggled to gain legitimacy in its contestations with market philosophies and values. Discovery 1 was much less established and certain of its own philosophy. While the policy documents, or actual policy, proclaimed the school's philosophy was discovery learning, this was contradicted by the micro-interactions, language usage and practices of the school's policy-in-use, which were shaped by traditional transmission pedagogies, or business discourses and practices from the world outside school.

Throughout the book other kinds of educational sites are introduced as cases of conditionally public entities like Sands or Discovery 1, with the main research sites from the context of English schooling and these cases supplemented with numerous examples from education systems within similar sociopolitical and national contexts. However, an important element of the book is to find broader truths within these specific examples. Bernstein's sociological tools are one means to bridge the gap between individual and social phenomena by revealing how experiences are regulated through repeated and rule-bound behaviours, passed on from one generation to the next through the grammar that regulates cultural transmission. Establishing meaningful relationships between the individual and the social, or the micro and macro, is one of the most significant concerns of sociology.

> Perhaps the most fruitful distinction with which the sociological imagination works is between the 'personal troubles of milieu' and 'the public issues of social structure'. This distinction is an essential tool of the sociological imagination and a feature of all classic work in social science. (C. Wright Mills 1970, 14)

In a book concerned with publics it is essential that it broaden its discussion from individual settings to public issues and social structure. For some decades sociological, and especially socially critical educational, research has been dogged by criticisms about the generalizability of its methodologies. While some educational sociologists concern themselves with macro issues, and longitudinal, quantitative methods, most educational research is conducted on a small scale, and through qualitative methods. Paradigm wars between qualitative and quantitative researchers, and public debates regarding the quality and usefulness of educational research are not significant to the topic of this book, and you can read my position on them in a discussion elsewhere on advancing the relationships between social theory and qualitative research (Boyask, 2012). As Mills points out, the significance of the personal to the public is a relationship critical to the discipline sociology. Many sociologists have developed robust methods for examining the socially significant through in-depth or case study methods. In addition to Bernstein, Michael Burawoy's (1998) articulation of a methodological duality of both positive and reflexive science in his elaboration of an extended case method is helpful to a pragmatic approach. Positive science is the normative construction of social science research, undertaken by a researcher detached from the world they observe and with the aim to mirror its reality. Positive methodology is typified through survey methods and underpinned by principles of reliability, replicability, representativeness and the negation of reaction or distortion of the world under study. Burawoy's extended case method makes no pretence to adhere to the principles of positive science, which is both its limitation and its strength. Instead he relates it to reflexive science, which is underpinned by an equivalent but different set of principles. In reflexive science the context effects that positive researchers minimize and control for, are 'not noise disguising reality, but reality itself' (Burawoy, 1998, p. 13). Instead of distance, the reflexive researcher seeks intersubjectivity between participant and observer, and comes to understand through dialogue. The principles underlying reflexive science are found in the antithesis of positive science, so that reactivity through mutual intervention in the research process is a virtue. Where positive science would seek certainty from a data point, to increase reliability, reflexive science enters into the subjective world of the research participant to develop situational comprehension which is extended out through theorization to describe social processes. Through the principle of structuration, the research reveals how social processes in the setting both shape and are shaped by an external field of social forces. Finally, reflexive science is underpinned by the principle of reconstruction to build the generality of the research, and therefore its significance. While a single case can never be representative of social phenomenon, its uniqueness is less important when the case is established to test out and elaborate upon existing social theory.

To summarize, the book's rationale for reconceptualizing public education by focusing upon individual sites is underpinned by a pragmatic methodology (Biesta and Burbules, 2003) that connects the personal, social and analytical (Mills, 1970; Burawoy, 1998). There is a resonance between personal connection to the sites and their significance in terms of educational reform and related forces of cultural, technological and economic globalization (Olssen, Codd and O'Neill, 2004; Tamboukou, 2012). While the main educational sites examined are located in England, they are compared with similar examples from countries such as New Zealand, Australia and the United States, which allows the book to highlight and question the Anglo-American imaginary that dominates global educational reform (Mundy et al., 2016). In these countries educational policies like Tomorrow's Schools (1989) reforms in New Zealand, Public Benefit Corporation legislation in the United States and academies programme in

England have blurred the lines between private and public education by not only promoting autonomy in some aspects of education governance but also requiring organizations retain links with government through financing or accountability for performance. In these conditions it is hard to define public education and understand its purpose. Throughout the book educational sites in England are analysed, compared with similar sites in other countries that have enacted neoliberal political reform through their education systems, and these analyses are used to produce contemporary and relational definitions of 'public' in commonly used terms like public accountability, public service, public benefit and public good as they are relevant to education.

The structure of the book

The book widens understanding of public education by drawing upon theoretical concepts of democracy and pluralist publics as well as investigation through empirical research. Some of the foundational theoretical ideas have been introduced in this chapter, especially problematizing understanding of the concept of the public within public education. Other related theories are set out in Chapter 2. The chapter takes as its starting point Dewey's (2016) powerful work *Democracy and Education*, in which he establishes a definition for education that is based in the growth of collective human capacity. Dewey's conceptualization of democracy helps us keep alive a vision of an interdependent society based in the deliberation, opinion formation and decision-making of its people, even while its collectivism is recognizably in contest with traditionalist and neoliberal concepts of power and government. The chapter builds upon this first chapter's introduction to the notion of pluralist publics to further refine the notion of public education, extending the public good of education to diverse groups that may be overlooked within an impoverished mainstream democracy. However, it also makes a realistic appraisal of the difficulties of translating democratic ideals into actually existing democracy. While it raises the possibilities of small, localized self-governing publics that exercise their interests through self-managing institutions it also recognizes the challenges they face in resisting normative and oppressive discourses conveyed through larger and more authoritative forms of government, such as the government of the neoliberal state. Dewey's answer for democracy undermined by authoritarianism of a nation state was the construction of the great community that brought publics back into the role of self-rule by strengthening their capacity for decision-making through education and improved access to systematic knowledge. International policy setting and its influence on national educational systems set a further challenge for public education. Present-day globalization affects public education, yet there is no global public to deliberate upon or make decisions on public education issues. For Fraser (2014), this strengthens arguments for transnational publics that can exercise transnational self-rule, despite eminent challenges facing existing and ideal democratic forms of transnational governance. From a Deweyan perspective the greater community is an interdependent and cohesive community. Fraser adds a critical edge to an ideal conceptualization of democracy, recognizing that actually existing plural publics exist in conditions of conflict and contestation. Both inform the conceptual position of this book because in combination there is a third alternative to perceiving democracy as an unattainable ideal or a fruitless perpetual struggle.

The problematization of common-sense understandings of public education continues in Chapter 3 by identifying concepts of publicness within what are more commonly understood as private and privatized educational entities. Categorical distinctions between public and private education located within public and private sectors are overly simplistic, and a better depiction of the educational field depends on more complex relational understandings of both public and private. The chapter continues the expansion of understanding of public education through opening up to public scrutiny and recognizing the public dimensions of private and privatized entities. That is, even private schools are regulated by the public either overtly through official legislation and policy, or covertly through the regulation of discourse. The publicness of private schools is highlighted initially through an analysis of private schools in England and their relationship with charity law. The purposes of charitable organizations throughout the United Kingdom and many other common law jurisdictions must be for public benefit. Most charities in England must demonstrate public benefit in their instruments of government and show its ongoing realization through annual reporting. While privatized, state-funded academy schools fall into an exempt category, private fee-charging schools are not exempt and the majority of them adopt charity status. Private schools that are charities recently have tested the definition of public benefit through the courts in England, responding to criticisms that guidance from the Charities Commission on what constituted public benefit was opaque. Guidance remains limited and coupled with the Charities Commission's restricted resources to regulate charities there is homogeneity in how England's private schools realize public benefit rather than the diversity that might be expected from schools removed from direct regulation by the state; yet innovation in how English private schools approach public benefit is very rare and beyond the legislative requirements most schools are subject to mimetic coercion in their organizational approach. There are some other ways private schools engage with the public. Private schools historically were associated with the bourgeoisie public sphere, because they offered an alternative to education within the home and through their expansion provided education of a wider group of the populace than ever before. Yet the main way that private interests are represented in England's education is through the privatization of state-funded education, and while study of privatization focuses on the expansion of governance by private interests, privatization is still the work of the state accountable to a national public. In their work on the rise of consultancies in England, Gunter and Mills (2017) identify four main ways that public services change through educational privatization: (1) expansion of the market through private providers, commissioned and controlled by the state; (2) an increase in private resources contributing to the funding base of educational services; (3) policy changes that respond to private interests such as policies of choice and individualization; (4) public sector services that are recast as in the interest of private individuals. A problematization of the private interests inherent in each of these scenarios means recasting them as engagement with public interests, albeit the impoverished public interests of a state governed by democratic and neoliberal discourses. So, for example, while some of these forms of privatization have affected state-funded schools, privatization has in the main affected them through the adoption of techniques of private governance rather than private ownership. Despite the erosion of public values in privatized schooling, state-funded compulsory education remains the gold standard for the education system of a legitimate nation state.

Some entities attempt to moderate the effects of market competition through taking on governance and legal forms that engage with concepts of the public either wholly or partially outside of the state sector. Chapter 4 draws from public sphere theory to define what counts as a public entity, disentangling the public from common-sense understandings such as 'the state' or 'the general public' and reconceptualizing the public in public education as pluralist, contextually specific and conditional (Fraser, 1990; Warner, 2002). It focuses on mapping the structures educational entities adopt, including their legal forms, ownership models and the regulatory fields in which they operate, and considers the extent to which they are limited as public entities. It identifies four different categories of entity: (1) entities that work towards social goals for the good of members using well-established, corporate structures (predominantly co-operative and mutual structures); (2) entities that adopt structures specially designed for organizations concerned with public benefit and not business, including charities that are forms with a long history as well as new public benefit organizations; (3) public–private partnerships where different partners have different goals and responsibilities in respect of profit-making, public benefit and risk; and (4) new kinds of entity such as social enterprise, for-profit and public benefit corporations that have been established with the intent to bring together public and private benefit. These entities share a commitment to social goals, mutual human relations or environmental ethics that extend beyond even as they engage with economic development. While their position is contentious and opens education up to market risk, they offer an alternative perspective on the decline of public education as the inevitable march towards a fully privatized education system.

The next three chapters engage with three concepts related to public education, that is, public benefit, public accountability and public service. These concepts change when the concept of public within them shifts from a normative concept of public, perhaps bounded by national citizenship status, to a concept of multiple, emergent publics that are defined through the exercise of governance through self-rule. The chapters explore these concepts both theoretically and through illustration from empirical studies of educational sites, which are private in the sense that they are removed from aspects of direct government control, yet demonstrate some features of a democratic public; that is, locations where groups of people participate in free and equal exchange, deliberation, opinion formation and decision-making (Dewey, 1916; Fraser, 1990).

Chapter 5 considers the public good of entities outside of the mainstream public sphere in the light of Chapter 4's typology. As shown in Chapters 3 and 4 a corporate structure does not disqualify an entity from working towards social goals, even though profit-making or corporate governance may result in compromises to public benefit. This chapter uses examples from universities' codes of conduct to suggest that the ethics of business may narrow the focus on what counts as the public good in profit-making entities, reinforcing sovereign rather than collectivist individualism. Similar struggles are explored in greater depth through examples of private schools. Tensions in pursuing a public good are examined in the context of some rare private schools that attempt to mitigate the anti-democratic qualities of the private schooling sector in England. These private schools aimed to promote equality and participation through some aspects of their operations. The chapter considers to what extent the governance structures within the schools support their aspirations and what this means for the public good more generally.

English private schools are accountable to the state under the Independent School Standards (2010), corporate law and the majority are accountable under the Charities Act, which requires them to demonstrate public benefit. The schools reported here have a commitment to the public good that extends beyond these limited accountabilities, demonstrating the weaknesses of the public good as it is presently defined by the state and also advancing understanding on the extent to which the schools may be regarded as Fraser's (1990) counterpublics. In all cases the schools compromised their democratic aspirations, but the extent to which this occurred varied. The chapter also continues the rationale for defining the 'public' in relation to private education by illustrating how publics exist in actual rather than ideal forms (Fraser, 1990), including within the private sector. Sometimes publics manifest in unanticipated places and forms, and these exceptional sites are interesting in their own right and also help us understand from a new perspective contemporary contestations and reformations of the public good and associated principles of equality, participation and social justice. Exceptional sites are especially important to examine when these important principles are marginalized within mainstream publics such as neoliberal national polities.

Public accountability in a marketized and individualized society seems a contradiction in terms. Yet a nuanced view of individualization that recognizes its potential association with democratic participation opens up a conversation that may be closed if individualism is only perceived as sovereignty of the individual will and not as a constituent force of society. Chapter 6 illustrates what public accountability might look like when we conceive of public spheres as multiple and polyvocal. It initially draws on theorization on the individualization of society (Beck, 1996; Yeatman, 2007), and then examines different concepts of the individual within one of the private schools that was also discussed in Chapter 5. In this case it is the democratic secondary school Sands, which illustrates the conditions of democracy when a school operates outside of the constraints of the actually existing public sector education. For Beck individuals are forced into roles of responsibility and held to account for crises that are outside of their control. Yeatman's conceptualization of a variety of individualisms provides a more optimistic view. She recognizes a political struggle between different forms of individualism. When Yeatman was writing in 2007 she saw at the centre of the struggle three main tactical moves of individualism underpinned by different conceptualizations of individuals: (1) a nostalgic attempt to revive a discredited patrimonial individual whose authority comes from sovereignty over a domain defined through private property assets (including women as chattels); (2) a democratic challenge to patrimonial individualism by individualisms diverse in form, creative in the constitution of their subjectivity and responsible to the collective; and (3) a postpatrimonial individualism of the will that has disarticulated itself from the restrictions of geography and gender and derives its authority through its own capital assets, and thus is paralleled in the radical and free-floating individual of neoliberalism. The research study provides a context in which to observe the struggle between individualisms. While traditional and postpatrimonial sovereign authorities are evident and at work, what is interesting in this context is that participatory and collectivist individualism remains the strongest form of subjectivity despite its situation in what is traditionally regarded as private sector schooling. Sands School provides an example of resistance to regulation from either the state or the market within an entity that sits outside of a mainstream and bounded public sphere yet still engages with the public in an ideal and democratic sense.

Sands is an unconventional site for examining public accountability because of its removed location from what is generally regarded as the public sector. A place where you would still expect to find notions of public accountability is within public service. In England local government had a significant role to play in maintaining the schooling system that has only recently been challenged with the expansion of semi-autonomous schools through academization. Yet the changes since the Academies Act 2010 have been profound. Chapter 7 shows the hasty retreat of four local authorities from the mainstream public through their adoption of policies of privatization. Each of these four authorities has committed to privatization, yet each enters into a qualitatively different relationship with the educational services market. One is overtly committed to supply-side economics in its attempt to lower costs through entering into partnership with a large logistics company. In its commitment to the corporate values of market exchange it adopts a position as business broker between service users (schools and families) and trading service providers. Another is also committed to market values yet expresses its commitment through localized innovation and scalable start-up initiatives. A third engages education community members in short-term contracts to deliver services, and the fourth had developed a catalogue of traded services within a business unit with the aim of developing a community interest company partnered with local primary and secondary headteacher groups. While the changes from public service provider to commissioner, broker or trader happened rapidly there remains significant variation between the local authorities in the philosophies underpinning their approaches. The differences in philosophy also show up to an extent in relations between the local authorities and the schools they serve.

Overall, the book argues for the complexity and elusiveness of publicness and rejects dichotomizing between market and state (Newman, 2007; Robertson et al., 2012) by focusing on how the public is defined in relation to private education. Through examining education as situated practice it aims to show how contemporary concepts of the public have been transformed and restricted through the growth of new relationships between the state and private education markets, or public–private partnerships. Yet the book goes beyond critique of private interests in education by opening them up to public scrutiny and recognizing when private entities exhibit public characteristics. It also highlights examples of counterpublic education in entities outside of mainstream public education that offer important, albeit imperfect, imaginings of a more equal or democratic world at a time when democratic publics are not readily supported within the mainstream.

Its arguments are developed from empirical case studies, as well as historical and recent social theory of 'public' applied to the public policy issue of public education. Some of these ideas have been introduced in this chapter, with the introduction of Habermas's ([1962] 1991) work on the deliberative public sphere of the bourgeoisie, theorization of government as a formal manifestation of public (i.e. parliamentary or democratic states are institutionalized forms of public), the polyvocal, multiple publics of Fraser (1990) that position the neoliberal state/publics as weakened mainstream publics and organizations outside of state as potentially stronger counterpublics. The relationships between economic exchange and government are also important elements to keep in focus, following Fraser's (1990) contention that while it is important for democratic theory to keep economy conceptually distinct from state apparatuses, we should not privatize economic exchange and exclude it from the scrutiny, deliberation and opinion formation that occurs within the public sphere. Yet, there are other threads of theory significant to the aims of the book. The critical theory of pluralist publics is examined alongside the socially democratic theory of Dewey in the next chapter.

Note

1 An educational public here is defined as a group of people who have come together for the purpose of education and are engaged in the work of a public, that is, political participation involving deliberation, opinion formation and decision-making through discussion and debate (Fraser, 1990; Habermas, [1962] 1991).

2

Theorizing Pluralist Public Education

Since education is a social process, and there are many kinds of societies, a criterion for educational criticism and construction implies a particular social ideal. The two points selected by which to measure the worth of a form of social life are the extent in which the interests of a group are shared by all its members, and the fullness and freedom with which it interacts with other groups. An undesirable society, in other words, is one which internally and externally sets up barriers to free intercourse and communication of experience. A society which makes provision for participation in its good of all its members on equal terms and which secures flexible readjustment of its institutions through interaction of the different forms of associated life is in so far democratic. Such a society must have a type of education which gives individuals a personal interest in social relationships and control, and the habits of mind which secure social changes without introducing disorder. (Dewey, 1916, p. 76)

The centenary of the publication of Dewey's *Democracy and Education* (1916) prompted considerable reflection of scholars on the relevance of the work for present-day public education (Boostrom, 2016; Gordon and English, 2016; Heilbronn et al., 2018). In *Democracy and Education* education is growth not just of the individual but an expansion of the collective in respect of its 'human powers and sensitivities' (Waks, 2017, p. 10). While Dewey is critical of schools contemporary to his writing, he reconceptualizes schooling as a public good that, more closely associated with the occupations of social groups, would provide a vehicle for the education of the democratic and ethical self (Biesta, 2016; Waks, 2017). In the phenomenon of modern-day compulsory schooling there is little common understanding of what constitutes a public good. The goals of compulsory schooling are contested (Labaree, 1997; Gerrard, Savage and O'Connor, 2017). Schooling like other public institutions and services have been dismantled through policies of modernization and privatization, and belief in collectivity and commonality in schooling has been severely shaken. Schools remain dependent on state funding in national education systems that have most enthusiastically adopted privatization of public services yet are substantially governed by private interests.

Like many other scholars I return to Dewey's influential work on democracy and education in this chapter. My aim is to understand how democracy and education are mutually constitutive. Recent scholarship finds many reasons to return to Dewey, ranging from a philosopher's recognition that Dewey's democratic engagement describes the continual redefinition of public schools as they readjust to changing circumstances (Gordon, 2016) to the influence of Dewey's democratic theory on a newly opened primary school from a head teacher's perspective (Higham and Biddulph, 2018). This scholarship is indicative of a strong desire within the field of education for equitable public schooling and related to what is explained by Gerrard (2015) as part of a generalized attempt to claim public education as a democratic resolution to the neoliberalization of schooling, based in a nostalgic remembering of a public education lost. As Gerrard suggests there never was such a public education. Its remembering can act as a rallying cry against the restrictions and inequalities of neoliberal schooling policy, yet contestations over the definition of public education, especially its public dimension, can serve to muddy the waters about what really constitutes the public good and what we expect of public schooling even among those jointly opposed to neoliberalism.

While Dewey's version of democracy includes decision-making through deliberative processes, it also depends upon the interplay and equality of difference. Neoliberal discourses that dominate contemporary schooling bear some relationship to concepts of democracy and the public good, particularly in respect of ideas about freedom and self-rule. The neoliberal versions are, though, shadow concepts in comparison to those associated with rich democracy and expansive human growth, because rather than a collective of diverse individuals their concept of freedom is bounded and limited to sovereign and not interdependent individuals. Take, for example, the concept of choice, one of the most pervasive discourses of contemporary school policy. While policies informed by choice are generally regarded as a form of privatization or retreat of state services from the public realm, they are not disconnected from democracy (Yeatman, 1996). Choice underpins a set of policy reforms that offer parents and students the opportunity to make decisions about educational provision as if customers. Decision-making is an important element of a democratic society, yet choice as a consumer decision is associated with public choice theory, which applies to problems of public policy a competitive market model of economics that regards all members of the public as consumers acting in their own interests. Public choice theory is related to a wider set of discourses that frame policy texts, including new contractualism, new public management, new institutional economics and rational choice. Public choice theory and its related policy discourses have been very influential in all aspects of public policy. Choice theory emphasizes the choice or consumption of services by a public service user, and therefore is individualistic, but at its heart lies a social relationship or contract between public service user and public service provider. While this is a restricted rather than fully collectivist sociality, contractualism in public policy and practice within democratic nation states is still the realization of an elected government's social obligation to the people. Policies of choice and contractualism in educational services are governed by market relations and therefore may appear to be outside of the scope of a book on public education, but conceiving contractualism as a public policy tool of an impoverished democracy keeps privatized educational institutions and services and policies of choice within the scope of public deliberative decision-making, which is where it needs to be.

Yeatman (1996) puts policies of choice under public scrutiny by making apparent their social basis. She argues that even while policies that prioritize choice individualize, they are also based in collectivity and social relations, because collective desire and belief in choice must act to unify in order to sustain the policy. What distinguishes this collectivity from other forms is that 'collective desires and beliefs exist only as they are mediated through individualised choice, consent, judgment and commitment' (1996, p. 45) and is therefore based in an assumption of individualism where individuals are conceptualized as isolated and autonomous. This differs markedly from a Deweyan conceptualization of the individual and social, where the presumption is that not only are individuals integrally connected to one another to make up society, but that individuals are reciprocally constitutive. Yeatman's (2007) work on varieties of individualism also conceives of mutually constitutive or collectivist individuals, an idea explored in Chapter 6, and shows that individualism does not have to fragment society.

However, school choice in education policy reform is more often associated with the autonomous choosing individual (Olssen et al., 2004). The autonomous individual is the service user conceptualized in typical school choice policies, such as the following policies in the United States: voucher and tuition tax credits, charter schools, homeschooling, interdistrict and intradistrict choice (choosing a school other than the one assigned), or recently burgeoning virtual or online schools (Miron and Welner, 2012). Policies of school choice, privatization and market-like educational governance (that often accompany choice) fragment national schooling systems because their underlying assumptions are that the foremost purpose of schooling is to fulfil the aspirations of individuals (Labaree, 2007). Choice contributes to a segregated and fragmented society because society frames individual choices not in consideration of common goals or beliefs about what constitutes the good for all but to achieve self-determination and maximization. While wider societal goals remain, these are orientated towards the desires and choices of the individual. Policies of state that prioritize the interests and decisions of individual consumers or service users are still connected to some concept of the public, but it is a very restricted vision of a democratic public when opinion is shaped by individualized desire. The relationships between consumer demand and public opinion are examined in this chapter and returned to in Chapter 5 where a case study in Sands school demonstrates complexities of public accountability in schools that negotiate between public opinion informed by both individual consumption and collective deliberation. However, the main goal of this chapter, and indeed the book, is to hold in mind an enriched notion of democracy with a deliberative and co-operative public, even while recognizing the restrictions of impoverished democracy. The main purpose of this chapter is to explore how a refined understanding of actually existing and pluralist educational publics can help to show that public education even in contemporary times is more than a dream lost to an impoverished mainstream democracy. A refined definition of the public in public education takes account of the instances of democracy that constitute public education and resists construing public education normatively in either its ideal or impoverished forms.

Contemporary Deweyan scholarship on democracy and education should help to clarify the purpose and nature of public education. Yet arguments for public education are not always clear on the nature of the public nor how through their vision for public education the best interests of the public will be served. An example of this is Fielding and Moss's (2010) argument for a radical democratic education through common schooling. They build a careful argument to explain the interplay between individual members of a democratic public through the philosophy of personalism and democratic participation in the public sphere through participatory or direct democracy. The rejection of representative democracy leaves this vision of common schooling open to challenge, suggesting that its practices of governance may be left to popular rather than informed opinion. That is, there are questions left open by Fielding and Moss related to the nature of knowledge and the role of experts in informing public opinion. As Feinberg (2012) points out in Dewey's conceptualization of the public in public education, he never examined nor defined in his major educational works *the public* educated in common schools, for him 'leaving the impression that a public is reducible to its individual members' (p. 6). In *Democracy and Education* Dewey (1916) tends to use the term public only to suggest commonality, which leaves the impression of a public unified in political philosophy and unitary in form. Characterizing the public in either of these ways is contrary to the main argument of Dewey's work that regards the interplay not just of individuals but also of different social groups as crucial to democracy.

Other scholars (Feinstein, 2015; Waks, 2010) have returned to Dewey's work to piece together a stronger articulation of the public in public education. The remainder of this chapter picks up the thread of this work to examine arguments for public education where the public is differentiated, plural and constituted socially, including through the social practice of democracy. It supports Dewey's democratic ideal as the fundamental purpose of education, whereby socially connected individuals develop their potential through free and equal exchange within their social groups, and through engagement with others unlike themselves. However, public education has developed differently from how Dewey envisaged, reflecting not just a departure from the ideal of the common school but also that the ideal must necessarily change to reflect the complexity of actually existing society.

Publics and their opinion

As discussed in respect of public education in Chapter 1, the public of public education also requires a more nuanced definition than is commonly used. Discussing public education in everyday discourse, its scope is often limited to its funding and resourcing arrangements, that is, education funded and managed by the state, and distinguished from private education, which is privately funded and managed. This characterization of public education is too simplistic on two counts. First, it is underpinned by an assumption that the public of public education is reducible to the state, a position entrenched through the term public sector where public schools reside. Second, the public is not unitary.

Taking up the first point, the public sphere needs to be disentangled conceptually from the state even though common usage and understanding show it is clearly related to the state. To understand the public, we need to establish how it differs from the state and how it is related to the state. In his reflection upon the structural transformation of the public sphere in relation to capitalism, Habermas (1991) recognized in the early phases of capitalism separations between the private individuals who came together as a public from the public authorities, or state. The private individuals and public authorities were drawn from a bourgeoisie elite in the Marxist sense, or those who have control of the means of production. The non-state bourgeoise public engaged in deliberation and debate on issues of public importance. As capitalism developed, the critical voice of the public influenced the political realm and became institutionalized into the modern parliament, allowing the public (constituted of private individuals) to legislate itself and therefore meet the democratic condition of self-rule. However, 'the public sphere in the political realm as an organ of state' (p. 81) did not encapsulate the totality of publics. A separate bourgeoise public sphere developed alongside parliamentary democracy, acting as space for political deliberation and debate and that informed state development and processes but was not reducible to them (Habermas, [1962] 1991). The public sphere:

> designates a theater in modern societies in which political participation is enacted through the medium of talk.
> This arena is conceptually distinct from the state; it a site for the production and circulation of discourses that can in principle be critical of the state. (Fraser, 1990, p. 57)

Distinguishing the public sphere and the state is an acknowledgement that even within a state that associates itself with democracy its actions may develop without consideration of the public will and in accordance with private rather than public interests. Neoliberal states may call themselves democratic and may take on some of the characteristics of democratic representation, yet if the preparation to participate in democracy or the formation of public opinion is limited a public may lack the capacity to participate in and evaluate public processes (Davies and Chong, 2016; Reeves and Loopstra, 2017).

In accordance with the second point, we can see that different publics exist at different times. Habermas differentiated public spheres historically, for example, that 'the theme of the modern (in contrast to the ancient) public sphere shifted from the properly political tasks of a citizenry acting in common (i.e., administration of law as regards internal affairs and military survival as regards external affairs) to the more properly civic tasks of a society engaged in critical public debate (i.e., the protection of a commercial economy)' (1991, p. 52), whereas in the twentieth century publics shifted from cultural-debating to a cultural-consuming public, informed in its judgements and tastes by the mass media. However, a conceptualization of publics less directly connected to a linear account of historicism permits these two forms of public to exist concurrently. While the dominant and mainstream conceptualization of public may indeed be a consumer-driven public, a pluralist conception of publics allows for the possibility of different publics where public debates continue to shape opinion and decision-making. Fraser's (1990) critique of Habermas's concept of publics picks up a pluralist and historically contingent conceptualization of public sphere and extends it through critique of his depiction of a patriarchal bourgeoise public. She and other feminists have extended publicness to multiple publics, drawing on the example of the woman's movement to show how women constructed alternative or counterpublic spheres, alternative to the mainstream and male-dominated public sphere described by Habermas. This critique differentiates publics on grounds more than just their temporal differences, including publics weak or strong in democracy, and subaltern or counterpublics where debates are shaped by discourses different from those circulating in mainstream public spheres. 'In stratified societies, like it or not, subaltern counterpublics stand in a contestatory relationship to dominant publics' (p. 70) and interrupt the conflation of public sphere and state.

The presence of counterpublics adds to the argument for the need to keep public conceptually distinct from state. Yet a strong demarcation between public and state is problematic. A public which attains sovereignty is a stronger form of public than one that forms opinions but has no capacity to transform these opinions into authoritative decisions. Thus, mainstream publics are strong in authority even when weak in equality and participation. Controversially for many in education who oppose policies of differentiated and specialized schooling, Fraser (1990) presents us with the possibility that strong publics exist within self-governing institutions, and as units of sovereignty alternative to the dominant public associated with the nation state. Yet this is an argument important in recognizing the otherwise hidden conditionally public qualities of local entities in a market-driven education system, and an important underpinning principle for arguments to extend public governance to transnational entities.

> One set of questions concerns the possible proliferation of strong publics in the form of self-managing institutions. In self-managed work-places, child care centers, or residential communities, for example, internal institutional public

spheres could be arenas both of opinion formation and decision-making. (Fraser, 1990, pp. 75–6)

Fraser's suggestion is provocative since self-managing institutions within education are more commonly associated with privatization and deregulated market relations than democratic publics and participation. Yet she herself recognizes that the suggestion for self-managed institutions leaves open the issue of accountability to larger, authoritatively stronger publics that may demonstrate more the characteristics of neoliberalism and self-interest than democracy and its principles of equality and social justice. She is also wary of how strong publics of self-governed and managed institutions might find coordination with other publics difficult, even when they act in accord with similar interests. Yet denying the possibility of multiple, locally derived and developed or alternative publics means privileging some interests over others.

The public–private dichotomy commonly used when talking about schooling are powerful terms 'frequently deployed to delegitimate some interests, views, and topics and to valorize others' (Fraser, 1990, p. 73). One of the most insidious effects of a polemical division between public and private schooling is that it relegates many of schooling's most complex economic relationships to the private sector, especially as privatization of education increases, and therefore places it outside of legitimate public scrutiny and debate. To address this concern, it is helpful to add to a conceptual distinction between public and state a distinction between the public and the market.

> The public sphere in Habermas's sense is also conceptually distinct from the official-economy; it is not an arena of market relations but rather one of discursive relations, a theater for debating and deliberating rather than for buying and selling. Thus, this concept of the public sphere permits us to keep in view the distinctions between state apparatuses, economic markets, and democratic associations, distinctions that are essential to democratic theory. (Fraser, 1990, p. 57)

A well-functioning public sphere is 'inter-imbricated' with state and economy and does not bracket off or privatize economic relations from the public sphere. A more careful appraisal of policy changes in education includes recognizing the publicness of different entities irrespective of their relationship with the market or state and taking more care when analysing the privatization of state education. Education writ large and schools, in particular, do not lend themselves to a true accountability to the market (Glatter, 2012). While many schools have become more 'business-like' to varying degrees they all remain accountable to the state, and therefore are accountable to the public as it is manifest within the state. Indeed, many suggest that through recent reform in English schooling central accountability and control has increased rather than decreased even while policies emerge that claim to increase school autonomy (Glatter, 2012; Hatcher, 2014). In England some schools have attempted to co-opt policies of school autonomy such as the academy and free school policies towards more democratic ends. The struggle faced by co-operative schools to work in accordance with the democratic principles of the co-operative movement described in Chapter 4 provides an example of how schools might be overwhelmed by the authority of public opinion with more political authority yet weaker in its public interest. Yet it is also important to retain a line of sight on educational entities that have become 'privatized' from the mainstream state sector and retain governance to a point by strong alternative publics. The uncommon school Sands introduced at the beginning of this book provides an example of a school that has weak ties to the mainstream public sphere institutionalized through the state. While mainstream policy discourses make an appearance in its practices, its position as a privately funded school helps to distance it from the mainstream and supports its governance by a strong alternative public, albeit a very small and restricted public.

One of the challenges for democracy in both its theoretical and actually existing pluralist forms is to establish whose opinion counts in informed decision-making. In weak publics, deliberation is focused upon the formation of opinion but without concomitant authority to translate opinion into decision-making. Publics are strengthened when the bodies that represent them make authoritative decisions based upon public opinion and enact 'the force of public opinion' (Fraser, 1990, p. 75). Feinstein (2015) discusses Dewey's (1922) reflection on the nature of the public in a review of Lippmann's (1922) book *Public Opinion*. According to Feinstein, Lippmann in this book and his later *The Phantom Public* had argued that the public could not exist, not because of an individual's innate incapability for deliberation and opinion formation but because the constraints of modern life limit individuals' capacity to know what is going on and collectively debate in an informed way. No one person can know all that is needed to be known to govern in a complex system (Feinstein, 2015). Dewey agreed with Lippmann inasmuch as he recognized the limits of public opinion within a complex society, but he did not support Lippmann's vision of a differentiated society where opinion formation occurred between the holders of specialist knowledge and the officials of state charged with safeguarding the public's interest but divorced from the public. He saw the challenge for democracy of informing public opinion as a challenge for education, especially through the communication to the public of organized knowledge. He develops his argument further in *The Public and Its Problems*:

> Dissemination is something other than scattering at large. Seeds are sown, not by virtue of being thrown out at random, but by being so distributed as to take root and have a chance of growth. Communication of the results of social inquiry is the same thing as the formation of public opinion. (Dewey, 2016, p. 198)

In Dewey's vision of democracy, the public rather than the state calls on experts to act on their behalf in securing their interests, and also to inform and transform their opinion. The representatives of the public who further the public interest through the state qua executive are therefore not only specialists in government, that is, politicians and policy officials, but also include all specialized roles such as 'expert school instructors, competent doctors, or business managers' (p. 155). In this version of democracy there is directness in the relationship between the public and state, but it is still a form of representational rather than direct democracy as the final decision-makers are public agents acting in accordance with public opinion rather than citizens themselves.

The greater community of the twenty-first century

Dewey emphasized the connectedness of citizens (Feinstein, 2015), and that their interrelationships transcend the limitations of individuals. Dewey (1916) was concerned that technological and industrial modernization had disarticulated citizens from the public sphere and their public roles through increased specialization and social complexity. In moving from local to national communities the public had ceased to recognize itself and its deliberative role in shaping society and state formation. He conceptualized the need of the great community that brought democracy to the modern society and state, reflecting its complexity and differentiation. Since Dewey was writing society has become more complex through advanced technological change and economic globalization. Public education reformers were influenced by policy developments in other nations (Mundy et al., 2016), as the expansion of compulsory schooling shows (Ramirez and Boli, 1987). Mundy et al. argue that more recent education policy reform goes beyond the policy borrowing of the nineteenth century and is shaped at national levels by sustained and organized international policy setting. The pluri-lateral agreements between states and supranational infrastructure such as the United Nations and OECD reflect that decision-making in twenty-first century globalism extends beyond the nation state, and to follow Dewey's line of reasoning democracy may require an even greater community of either global or transnational proportions.

While tensions between global and local interests have put to bed any truly global public sphere, Fraser (2014) argues that the idea of a transnational public sphere that operates beyond the nation state boundaries has become accepted in common parlance, especially when talking about arenas for communication that cross national boundaries. Whether these function as public spheres in the democratic sense is less than clear. Public opinion acquires legitimacy and political efficacy in a critical theory of democracy only if participants are legitimately constituted as a public. The presupposition of democracy is that it is a self-referential political system, that is, political power is exercised through collective self-rule, yet this premise presents challenges when the public extends beyond national boundaries as in a transnational society. Where are the boundaries of a transnational public?

Many modern democrats, and indeed Dewey (2016), delineate the public through a democratic all-affected principle, where 'having one's interests affected intrinsically grounds a right of democratic say' (Abizadeh, 2012) and confers citizenship on the affected. Dewey (1916) was critical of associating democracy with nationalism, where democratic rights were conferred by national citizenship, and its involvement in a conceptualization of education, which he claimed '… narrowed the conception of the social aim to those who were members of the same political unit, and reintroduced the idea of the subordination of the individual to the institution' (p. 76). Yet there is confusion and debate within actual national democratic polities as to whether citizenship is conferred by the effect of government, or by membership of a nationality or ethnicity that predates government (giving rise to nationalist or separatist governments). Furthermore, when the all-affected principle is applied to establish the limits of a national citizenry it produces 'fickle boundaries' (Karlsson, 2006) and makes it hard to judge legitimacy. Legitimate boundaries of the people in the governance of transnational relations are even harder to discern, where there is less clarity about who has a legitimate right to participate and who constitutes the public.

An alternative way to identify the public in transnational democracy is the application of the all-subjected principle (Karlsson, 2006; Fraser, 2010; Abizadeh, 2012). Under this principle the boundary of a public is defined by subjection to law. In discussing the limits of justice, Fraser (2010) says that all those who 'are subject to a given governance structure have moral standing as subjects of justice in relation to it' and defines the limits of the people that self-rule as 'their joint subjection to a structure of governance that sets the ground rules that govern their interaction' (p. 65). While the effect of state legislation on its citizens is the obvious example of being subject to the law, Fraser suggests that what counts as a governance structure can be conceived broadly to encapsulate more than just mechanisms of state and includes different local, regional, national and transnational agencies. Subjection is also conceived broadly to include many varieties of coercive power. The all-subjected principle and its use in defining the public of democracy is further theorized by Abizadeh (2012), who argues that the boundaries of the public are constituted through the practice of self-rule. That is, the public is in principle unbounded until it is constituted through the act of democratic governance. For the purposes of defining the public in public schooling, defining the public through a principle of subjection provides a much more nuanced picture of what counts as public schooling than the commonly used but heavy-handed distinction between public and private sector education. It is also a more inclusive definition, recognizing that boundaries are not drawn according to some pre-legitimizing criteria.

Who is the public in public schooling?

The history of public schooling generally starts with the history of compulsory schooling, or in its later formation as what Ramirez and Boli (1987) term 'mass schooling'. They locate mass schooling's origins in Western Europe, with the first regulations for a compulsory education appearing in the German state of Weimar in 1619 with its wider ambitions met in eighteenth-century Prussia of providing schooling en masse to all children, not only of the elite. Compulsory education entered the discourse and policy of Austria, Sweden, Denmark, Italy and eventually France and England, the dominant European powers at the time. Ramirez and Boli explain that similar compulsory education systems spread throughout Europe 'because this organizational strategy was the course of action most consistent with the developing Western European model of a national society' (p. 3). The United States of America differs in its political processes from many European countries, but, on a societal level, shares a similar conceptualization of state. Notably a mass schooling system developed in the United States to prepare a citizenry to contribute to its democratic statehood. Horace Mann's influential reports of 1837–1848 that set out a proposition for public schooling in America was influenced by the European models of mass schooling. Mann's (1957) underlying principles for public schooling were recognizably democratic, that is, freedom of access and provision of common experience to foster familiarity and fraternal feelings among children who may live in proximity to one another yet be quite unlike in other ways.

These principles underpinned the development of many modern state school systems and are evident today even though they may be enacted in less than ideal forms. According to UNESCO's statistical release that accompanies their 2019 Global Education Monitoring Report, 73 per cent of the world's 209 countries recognized by the United Nations have legislated for nine years or more of compulsory primary and secondary schooling. Compulsory schooling is not always free, as according to UNESCO only 50 per cent of the total countries have developed laws guaranteeing free education as a basic right. Putting aside until the next section of this chapter the contradictions of semi-autonomous schools that are state funded but privately governed (the most commonly recognized are free schools in Sweden, academy schools in England, charter schools in the United States, but others include direct subsidy scheme schools in Hong Kong and independent public schools in Western Australia), even mainstream state-funded schools are not always free, and some request parents pay a fee either overtly or through donations or extracurricular activities. Setting and streaming policies within schools can mean the experience of school is not common. Some admissions systems do not use proximity to the school as a fundamental criterion for entry, for example, schools with admissions that include a mixture of local and ballot entry. Mixed economies in public schooling that blend public and private interests are associated with wider discourses of techno- and economic rationalism. In this conceptualization, public schooling is an instrument applied by the state to the aim of social efficiency and economic productivity. Common in contemporary education policy is rhetoric on the contribution of the state schooling system to a nation's global competitiveness, achieved through varied forms of privatization of state services and assets (Boyask, 2015a), public–private partnerships (Robertson et al., 2012) and new public management (Anderson, 2017), all underpinned by neoliberal ideologies. In other words, public schooling is becoming more private. The responses from a socially critical perspective in support of public schooling to this changed environment have tended to approach from two lines. First, there is the critique of the neoliberalization of public schooling. This has been an extensive area of scholarship which has highlighted the changing concepts of society and individuals associated with globalization and economic rationalism that have spread to influence educational policies and practices (Mundy et al., 2016). Second is the adoption of public education in its ideal sense as a symbol to stand in stark contrast to the inhumanity of neoliberalism (Gerrard, 2015).

A third approach is emerging in the literature and is differentiated from the former two positions because, like the notion of responsibility for England's academy school leaders in Keddie's (2018) paper, it offers a 'counter-story' to the inclination to view existing policy and practice within privatized public schools solely through a neoliberal lens. Gerrard (2017) describes the public in public schools in Australia and claims that 'what is "public" is essentially contested, mutable and unbounded, connected to shifting claims of what is common' (p. 57). This is an emergent public, self-organized and 'created by the reflexive circulation of discourse' (Warner, 2002, p. 62). The unbounded public is evident in Abizadeh's (2012) demos, the democratic citizenry who are legitimate participants in the formation of public opinion through the practice of self-rule. The democratic public may be mutable and open to contestation, yet it is not unrestrained. The all-subjected principle applied to the demos means that its legitimate members are subject to the regulation of governance. In a deliberative democracy what is common is what is agreed to be common through the deliberation of the demos. Taking further Dewey's position on the role of the public, it is not to use deliberation to establish the rule of law but to be informed enough to appoint experts to carry out that role on its behalf and in its interests, and for them to further inform their opinion on future law and appointing the lawmakers who will be needed to establish it. Furthermore, Dewey's reflections on community suggested that the ideal common school, such as the one described in Mann's vision for public education, is an institution conceptualized for the interests of a simple and localized community. He reasoned that the nation state, or greater society, lacked community and therefore a public. The community of the nation state needs to reflect the greater specialization of a complex society yet retain coherency through interconnections and relationships. A complex and differentiated society and its plural, overlapping communities need a differentiated common school. Elsewhere (Boyask, 2013) I argued that Dewey's differentiated society was the kind of society envisaged by Durkheim, with its cohesion based in principles of equality between differences, and that a differentiated school system would not be out of place in such a society. This vision is resonant with Fraser's (1990) conceptualization of the public not as a unitary entity but as plural publics in existence through subjection to different laws emanating from different structures of governance. Yet there are significant differences. Dewey's greater community is harmonious and interconnected. Fraser's plural publics may exist in conflict and contestation with one another, even as she strives towards deliberation. In the combination of them both is an alternative to perceiving democracy as an unattainable ideal or a fruitless perpetual struggle.

The uncommon public school

School choice is one of the features of the global education reform movement that Sahlberg (2014) claims has emerged from the informal but sustained globalized exchange of education policy and practice. Central to school choice policies is an assumption that parents choose from a range of alternatives the best school for their children. While much has been written on the efficacy and inefficacy of school choice policies, their relevance to this argument is that their enactment results in a proliferation of school type. England is an extreme example of how policies formulated on principles of parental choice have markedly increased the types of schools: for example, recent school types include converter academy schools, sponsored academy schools, free schools, studio schools, university technical colleges and so on. However, school choice policies are only apparently about offering parents a choice. While the policies for diversity of school type appear to be about differentiation, as they become embedded in schooling practice schools become more alike. One way that standardization of schooling occurs is through national and international testing regimes (Sahlberg, 2014), where the high stakes of the assessments means teaching to the test takes priority over curriculum. Inspection regimes such as Ofsted and Estyn standardize schools. And yet another form of standardization occurs through privatization (West and Bailey, 2013; Glatter, 2017). In countries as diverse as United States, England and Sweden their governments have contracted private bodies to govern, manage and deliver schooling (West and Bailey, 2013). In England academy and free schools are connected through chains under private, charitable trusts, and quite often formed of different types of school. Yet the variety in school type does not necessarily result in differences in outcomes. 'Within such a structure the individual units become in effect sites for the delivery of education, rather than self-standing schools' (Glatter, 2017, p. 118).

United States' charter schools, England's academy schools and Sweden's free schools are each a form of uncommon schooling. They are regulated and funded by the state, but not on the same terms as other state-funded schools, with relative independence in governance and management and to an extent curricular and assessment decisions. Using the terminology of the OECD (2009), these schools have autonomy with public accountability. Some have reflected on the possibilities to use uncommon school frameworks for a democratic education (Knight Abowitz, 2001; Waks, 2010; Boyask, 2013). Might they be a democratic uncommon alternative?

Following Fraser (1990) the public sphere can be conceptualized as multiple, constructed of weak, strong, dominant and counterpublics. This argument has been explored before within the context of privatized schooling, asking whether the semi-autonomous charter schools of the United States constitute atypical, subaltern publics or no publics at all (Knight-Abowitz, 2010; Waks, 2010). In a series of symposium papers, Knight Abowitz (2010), Wilson (2010) and Waks (2010) explore the democratic potential of American charter schools, starting from the position that publics are pluralist, and therefore charter schools might represent the interests of different publics. Following this line of thought the opinion of a public, potentially a counterpublic whose voices are excluded from mainstream discourse, would lie behind the construction of a school charter. To return to Dewey's perspective on the role of the public, democratic charter schools would act as public agencies operated by educational specialists on behalf of its public with the purpose of informing public opinion. In support of democratic charter schools, Waks (2010) states: 'authorizing them as public agents grants an extra measure of public legitimacy and provides an additional instrument (for example, the charter school) for public action, bringing forth additional speakers and actors: parents, sponsors, school leaders, teachers, and students' (p. 667). Yet the three symposium authors acknowledge that the reality is somewhat different from the conceptualization of charter schools as an instrument of strong democratic publics, and that in the States that have adopted charter school policy there is evidence that they have exacerbated social segregation (Wilson, 2010). This is not the case with academy schools in England, where academy schools are not conclusively contributing to segregation, but they have not alleviated it either (Gorard, 2014). This is failure of their original goal to address the underachievement of children from low socio-economic backgrounds.

We might conclude therefore not to tinker with school type and avoid the failure of justice, that is, social segregation, by making schools more alike (Gorard, 2014). Yet this position does not consider that the problem of academy schools may not be that they need to be more like mainstream schools, but that they already are.

> The old saying that the cure for the ills of democracy is more democracy is not apt if it means that the evils may be remedied by introducing more machinery of the same kind as that which already exists, or by refining and perfecting that machinery. (Dewey, 2016)

It may not be system-wide reform that is at fault but the failures of a failing system that appears to reform but in effect standardizes. In the case of England's academies, the schools were perceived as individual units and only connected through quasi-market relations (Glatter, 2017). The schools compete with one another through league tables and market branding. This bears little similarity to the schools envisaged in a Deweyan differentiated society but is quite like England's mainstream schools. The main identifiable difference between academy and other state-funded schools usually cited is their governance arrangements, with academies run by private trusts, and the majority of other schools maintained by the local authority. Even after significant reform, England's local authorities are charged with upholding the public good through their oversight of many maintained schools, and even retain some responsibilities for academy schools. Yet how they discharge this responsibility has changed considerably. Many local authorities have adopted privatized systems of public service, entering into public–private partnerships or provision of services modelled on corporate lines (Boyask, 2015a). The conceptualization of the public sphere that underpins the privatization of local government and its educational services is one that conflates public with state, 'informed by the discipline of economics, which contrast the "market" to the "state"' (Robertson et al., 2012, p. 4). The more culturalist views outlined earlier in this chapter recognize the contested and historically located nature of the public sphere (Habermas, [1962] 1991; Fraser, 1990).

The state has acted both to promote the interests of the public (in the sense of the public at large) and also to perpetuate many forms of exclusion and oppression, creating paradoxical and fluctuating conditions for social justice. Such paradoxes are highlighted in a neoliberal state, where social obligation is mediated by individualized consent within contractual arrangements (Yeatman, 1996), making individuals who lack the capacity to make choices for their own advantage vulnerable to injustice. A differentiated school system based upon choice is not going to deliver on justice for those unable to choose what is in their best interest.

For the uncommon school to function as an instrument of justice it needs to fulfil the basic presumptions of justice. For example, Knight Abowitz (2010) defines under what conditions charter schools might work as agencies of plural publics, with responsibility for educational justice to their own and other interrelated publics:

> As I have delineated, the overall aim of publicly funded schools that serve both intrapublic and interpublic purposes for educational publics should be to prepare students for participatory parity as adults. This parity requires that schooling policies, structures, and curricula be shaped in light of four moral and political principles of justice: recognition, redistribution, representation, and transmission. (p. 701)

That is, if the premise of a school's existence is not justice but individual gain even those committed to social justice will struggle to enact it. What remains interesting about charter, academy and other autonomous schooling in a discussion on the public in a market-driven education is understanding to what extent policies, and the structures and curricula they frame, can be reinterpreted in alignment with principles of social justice. An example examined in a later part of this book is England's local authorities under England's Academies Act (2010). Cuts in bulk funding and the reallocation of funding to academy trusts established through central government policy mounts pressure on England's local authorities to relate to schools solely through market relations, that is, through brokerage, service provision or quality assurance, yet some local authorities try to resist the position they are forced into and adapt their business-like practices to a social ethics.

Some groups adopt and adapt the uncommon school structure as a means to achieve justice for those who have experienced oppression within a common schooling system. An example of this was the adoption by some in the indigenous Māori population of New Zealand's version of an autonomous state-funded school, partnership schools or kura hourua. Kura hourua were introduced in 2012 by a government that favoured school choice policies and were disestablished in 2018 by a left of centre, progressive government. The legacy of the British Crown's colonization and its commandeering of resources in Aotearoa New Zealand has left Māori in a position of marginalization within their own land. While a Māori-language immersion system of schooling has been established in parallel with mainstream schooling since the Education Act (1989), some groups of Māori seized upon the newer kura hourua as a vehicle to educate their children who are not already steeped in te ao Māori (the Māori world) in a 'culture of high expectation fostered in these alternative learning environments' in contrast to 'the negative cognitive bias against Māori and

Pacific students in mainstream classrooms' (Stoddart-Smith, 2018, ¶6). The disestablishment of partnership schools kura hourua in December 2018 was accompanied by significant protest from the communities they served.

Given what Fraser (2008) calls the abnormality of the times in respect of justice, we need to make sure that the enactment of justice we are looking for is not overly idealist and therefore dismissive of imperfect means for enacting any of these four principles of justice. Fraser calls for a theoretical framing of justice similar to the methodological framing of positivist and reflexive science discussed in Chapter 1 (Burawoy, 1998). In Fraser's case, she argues for a balance between recognizing limits to justice without bringing to a standstill rulings on justice. We need a theory of justice 'that is *simultaneously* reflexive and determinative' (2008, p. 407). In relation to the uncommon school as it exists as academy, charter or free schools, my position is that while critiques of their limits and restrictions on justice are essential to building fairer and more equal education, we concurrently need to understand, acknowledge and make just rulings about their continuance and support when schools are attempting to enact or, in some cases, are achieving some type of justice through their existing structures and forms.

Conclusion

When considering the nature of the public in public schooling, a more nuanced definition of public is a stronger and more inclusive definition. The dichotomy of public–private against which public schooling is most often defined is simplistic, and it leaves out many different voices from public opinion and delegitimizes valid public interests. Furthermore, this public sphere is weak in that its deliberative practices are confined to the formation of public opinion. Decision-making occurs elsewhere, and not only within the state which in many cases contracts out its responsibilities to private individuals and entities irrespective of public opinion. A strong public sphere gives voice to opinions that influence the authoritative decisions of its agents. Conceptualizing the public of public schooling as pluralist increases the range of interests legitimately included in public schooling and potentially improves participatory parity in citizenship.

Pluralist publics also better reflect the complexity of twenty-first century society, with its tensions between regionalisms, national boundaries and transnational mobilities. In this environment standardization of form even in the interests of justice is not a realistic goal for public education. Reflecting on the changes industrialization had wrought, Dewey recognized the need for specialization in a complex society. By the mid-twentieth century the critical theorists had identified a profound shift in society, from a culture-debating society to a culture-consuming society (Habermas, 1991). In a consumer society public opinion is formed through passive consumption of mass media, rather than active debate and deliberation. The spread of educational choice policies and their differentiated school systems is an excellent example of the influence of consumerism in public education. Yet while these systems may appear to be constructed in the public interest, public opinion formed through consumption is weaker than public opinion formed through deliberation. Self-managed organizations, in which we might include self-governing schools, may act as agencies of strong counterpublics. This framework, however, positions such organizations outside of mainstream and weaker publics, where public opinion carries less force and state regulation is dominant. As we shall see in further and elaborated examples of conditional counterpublics, which self-rule outside of mainstream publics, many struggle to enact their values in the face of stronger and more authoritative publics informed by weaker public opinion and therefore open to co-option by more powerful private interests. Yet injustices in self-governed schools in a school choice system does not mean we must give up on a differentiated school system.

3

Opening a Window on the Private Sphere

In the previous chapter I made a claim for the reconceptualization of privatized, autonomous schools as potentially strongly democratic self-governing institutions. Given the strength of competitive individualist discourses in school choice policies, the pursuit of a similarly differentiated school system built instead upon principles of democracy and justice can seem idealist. Dewey (1916) recognized limits to idealist thinking but argued that 'the democratic ideal of education is a farcical yet tragic delusion except as the ideal more and more dominates our public system of education' (p. 98). The contribution of this book to building a system of schools based on a socially democratic rather than individualistic neoliberal ideal is to look for and make visible the public in places where it may not be expected. Opening the window on conditional publics and their associated organizations in market-driven education opens them to public scrutiny and debate and may contribute to shifting discourse towards democracy and related principles of equality and justice. As long as it is a realistic appreciation of their imperfections, recognition of imperfect democratic publics in places where they are unexpected disrupts a pessimistic discursive field and opens up possibilities to broaden and deepen democratic discourses. The purpose of this chapter is to problematize the simplistic distinction between private and public education by finding the public interests in private spheres. Through scrutinizing private education from the perspective of public interests we find some conditional publicness, where alternative discourses circulate, and where democratic discourses openly compete with the regulatory or oppressive discourses of the state and/or market.

I have already identified a range of policy types that have been associated with school choice in the United States including voucher and tuition tax credits, charter schools, homeschooling, interdistrict and intradistrict choice, and virtual schools (Miron and Welner, 2012). Most but not all of these categories have an association with state sector education, but any of them might provide the ground where one might look for a conditional public given their underlying principles of consumer choice. However, the focus in this book is on educational entities, which might be individuals but more usually are organizations, institutions or networks that have obligations and rights, and through governance structures subject individuals to governmental power. This excludes voucher or tax credits which represent a contract between entities but may include the schools that accept them or lose students as a result of their deployment. What I am looking for are entities that to some extent are shaped and governed by the opinion of the publics that they subject. While I might have chosen just to focus on state-funded schools (that are commonly recognized as public schooling) as an example of organizations that might fit my criterion for inclusion, what I want to break down is an assumption that schools generally, and state-funded schools in particular, should be regarded as special kinds of institution for the education and preparation of publics. From a Deweyan perspective democratic education is essentially interconnected with the world it inhabits, whereas schools are more generally constructed as institutions bounded and set apart.

> That we learn from experience, and from books or the sayings of others *only* as they are related to experience, are not mere phrases. But the school has been so set apart, so isolated from the ordinary conditions and motives of life, that the place where children are sent for discipline is the one place in the world where it is most difficult to get experience. (Dewey, 1915, pp. 14–15)

The empirical research that informs this book not only includes investigation in state-funded schools but also touches on other entities that have an educational remit including the educational remit of local government, educational services that may or may not be provided by local government, private schools and their networks. Drawing upon cases from beyond state schooling decentres state schools as the singular locus of educational experience and recognizes the governmental effects on the education and opinion formation of individuals from other types of entity. It also provides a useful point of departure from which to consider how different types of entity interact with and influence one another. This is crucial to Dewey's democratic ideal, which is dependent upon not just the interplay between diverse and equal individuals but also the interplay as equals between different social groups. However, it also provides a profound critique of public policy that attempts to minimize social effects and emphasize individual effects. As Wright Mills (1970) signalled, the personal problems faced by individuals oftentimes have social origins and social solutions, and the revelations of social science show how all kinds of entities interact and are mutually constitutive of one another. For example, the Westminster government's Academies Act (2010) brought changes to England's state-funded schools and now approximately half have separated from the administration of the education arm of local government and become academies, governed either by standalone or multi-academy trusts. A public information release from the Department for Education revealed that by October 2018, 50.1 per cent of all state-funded school students were studying in a free or academy school, for the first time reaching over half of school students (DfE, 2019b). The changes have not just affected academy schools but have knock-on effects for local authorities through loss of funding, changes to the model of services they provide or commission and even schools that have elected to remain under local authority control. The extensive changes as a result of the Academies Act 2010 to both local authorities and schools are examined in Chapter 7. The change in status was most actively embraced by secondary schools, yet the change in governance also has an impact on their contributing primary schools, with some secondary academies more actively courting primaries through the offer of services, facilities or activities to build obligatory relationships that secure or open up new sources of enrolment. To focus on individual entities or even regional authorities and their relationship with a national education system, however, overlooks the increasingly important influence of entities that sit outside of national educational systems.

While Chapter 4 maps out the different kinds of entities where one might find conditional publics, this chapter takes a broader view to reconsider private and privatized educational entities that are generally discounted from discussions of public education. While the definition of public education is worked upon throughout the whole of this book, private education also is a complex phenomenon that is poorly served when the 'private' in private education is understood narrowly and in terms of its opposition to a narrowly conceived public education. Like public education, private education tends to be understood in terms of its funding basis, that is, funded by a means other than state funding. However, it is hard to sustain that definition given the many historical and contemporary examples of state funds allocated to private schools (i.e. private schools understood as private traditionally). For example, the Australian federal and state governments have a long history of funding non-government schools throughout the country, and well before the introduction of Western Australia's Independent Public Schools initiative in 2009, which like academy and charter schools are independent schools in a public education system.

The remainder of the chapter problematizes narrow definitions of private and privatized education to consider how public scrutiny of education governed by private interests allows us to open up the definition of what might count as public education. In the following accounts of private and privatized education we consider how private entities are regulated by and intersect with public interests, highlighting the public spaces which open up in the contradictions of private education. These contradictions are even more pronounced in privatized education, which is generally understood as the retreat of the state from the public realm. Here both private and privatized education are examined for their potential as conditionally public education.

Private education

Problematizing distinctions between public and private is a common topic in writing on both public and privatized education. The terms public and private in respect of education and other social phenomena are 'notoriously difficult to define' (Wilson, 2012, p. 18) because their meanings change according to their political and cultural context. While there are no essential meanings of the terms public and private, differences in their meaning take on importance and become established through common use. We might think about the use of these terms in two distinct ways. They exist in linguistic use as substantive categories in and of themselves ('the public' and 'the private'). They are also important modifying adjectives, and commonly used to distinguish different kinds of entity or concept (ibid.). Wilson uses the examples of type of institutions (public or private school), spatial metaphors (public or private spheres or sectors) and a sense of interest (public interests or private self-interests). Yet there are other expressions of different orders where 'public' is adopted as a linguistic modifier, including some examined in this book such as public opinion, public benefit and public accountability. In his influential article on the meaning of privatization Starr (1988) suggests that behind the meanings we attribute to such terms are conceptual pairings of public and private. That is, we define public in relation to private and vice versa even when the other term is not referred to directly. He claims that in our thinking we dichotomize public and private each time we make use of one or both terms; and that there are two main differences or dichotomies in the use of the terms.

> At the core of many uses are the two ideas that public is to private as open is to closed, and that public is to private as the whole is to the part. In the first sense, we speak of a public place, a public conference, public behavior, making something

public, or publishing an article. The private counterparts, from homes to diaries, are private in that access is restricted and visibility reduced. (p. 7)

On the other hand, when we speak of public opinion, public health, or the public interest, we mean the opinion, health, or interest of the whole of the people as opposed to that of a part, whether a class or an individual. Public in this sense often means 'common,' not necessarily governmental. (pp. 7–8)

The dichotomous pairings of open/closed and whole/part that Starr claims underpin the usage of public and private can be related to regular and prevalent contemporary and recent debates on education. In a discussion of public–private partnerships, Robertson et al. (2012) argue that while it is often overlooked, the public of public education is indicative fundamentally of its relationship and contribution to the public good. In this argument we might see the pairings in operation. In common usage public education is linked to the whole because its outcomes are inherently in the interest of all people, not just those who benefit as individuals. For example, in a discussion on the purpose and goals of American education, Labaree (1997) employed a notion of public that applies to the whole of the people, and private for the part. He maintained education was a public good whether it set out to achieve either good citizens through an approach to schooling based on the principles of democratic equality or economically productive units through an approach to schooling based on principles of social efficiency; and he argued against the injustice of conceptualizing education as a private good for competitive advantage and social mobility where only a part of the people gain benefit. Labaree's argument helps to clarify the underpinning principles of policy directives. Policies that promote social mobility are regularly promoted in the political sphere as a means to achieve social justice, yet his argument reveals an intrinsic unfairness in achieving mobility because it comes at the expense of others. Furthermore, it recognizes that policies that focus on economic productivity may not be as antisocial and individualistic, that is, associated with a private good, as they are sometimes understood. They are based on a contributory view of society, albeit, an impoverished view of society and the social roles needed for it to function because their relationships to the whole are framed by an economic discourse rather than the richer discourses of human potential in democratic equality. However, a limitation of his work is that it is based in a categorical distinction between public and private.

While Robertson et al.'s (2012) argument can be linked to the public–private dichotomy of open and closedness they also problematize clear distinctions and show how the public good might to an extent be served by private interests that are deemed to be closed off from the public realm. They point out that public education systems have historically been constituted in part through private contributions made by 'families, civil society and through the business sectors' (p. 2). Through their participation individuals benefit from democracy, and therefore a schooling system that is constituted as a democratic public good can concurrently be conceived as a private good. If public education is therefore a contested and problematic term that is not clearly distinct from private interests, then can the same be applied to private education? The prior quote from Robertson et al. gives a hint of the complexity that underlies concepts of the private as they relate to education. The private of private interests may refer to individuals, families, non-state institutions or communities or, as commonly perceived, businesses. Further diversity can be found within all these forms. A small local business is quite different in structure and ethos from a large multinational corporation, and families are positioned differently from one another according to their social, financial and cultural capital. Yet how we have come to understand private education is largely through a lens of economic capital, that is, on the basis of its funding arrangements. Private education is closed off from the public by restricting access to only those who can afford to pay the fees. This association seems to be based in an empirical reality, at least in respect of private education in England. Despite the potential diversity in what might count as private interests, the private interests in the private education of England are remarkably similar. In a study on democratic equality in private schools I examined all the available websites of private schools in England (1,711 of 1,924 schools had websites with enough information to make review possible, this was the total number in the survey) across the dimensions of governance, curriculum, pedagogy, school intake and outcomes (at societal, school and student levels) (Boyask, 2015b). The focus of the study meant what I looked for were schools that expressed through their website a commitment to democratic equality in any or all of these dimensions of schooling. Only sixty-four of the schools were deemed to meet the criteria for inclusion, and none of them met the criteria across all five dimensions. What was readily apparent was that democratic equality was a very weak political driver among private schools in England. Arguments against the involvement of private interests in education governance point to the limits of innovation in the private sector. The traditional view of the private sector in the fields of economics and business studies is as a prodigious innovator that reacts nimbly and with novelty to market demand. Mazzucato (2013) points out that most of the research and development that makes innovation in the corporate sector possible is originally funded by and originates from the state. This problematizes a view of the state as slow-moving and conservative, and Mazzucato's contribution to public versus private debate makes an argument for reconceptualizing the state as a progressive and entrepreneurial force. This argument is interesting to reflect on in light of the innovations in self-governing schools or privatization of schooling within the state sector. Yet the important point for this part of the discussion is that while the private sector is potentially diverse and innovative, schools tend to take on forms like one another.

Organizational convergence is a phenomenon recognized in organization studies, and notably termed institutional isomorphism by Di Maggio and Powell (1983). They argued that institutions become more like one another through coercive, mimetic or normative processes of isomorphism that occur through the structuration of related organizations. Structuration here refers to the interplay between structure and agency, whereby individuals and social structures are mutually constituting. Organizational structuration refers to the establishment of an organizational field through the interrelationships and structuring effects of related organizations. That is, through structuration an organizational field becomes more established and more clearly bounded, and organizations become less diverse and more similar in their forms and practices. Organizational rationalization of this type is often associated with the spread of market competition, and Di Maggio and Powell cite sociologist Max Weber as the source of this argument. Even though the rational outcome of competition for organizations is for them to establish points of difference and seek competitive advantage over one another, they actually tend to become more similar. At a societal level the intended outcome of competition among organizations is increased efficiency and productivity; however, even that tends not to be the case. Di Maggio and Powell argue that the driver for convergence is not continual improvement within organizations but a more general process of structuration that embeds structural relations of dominance and coalition within an organizational field, and these relations constrain difference in form and practice of organizations. 'But, in the long run, organizational actors making rational decisions construct around themselves an environment that constrains their ability to change further in later years' (p. 148). The rationalizing decisions made within organizations may have as their goal efficiency, diversity and improvement, but the main motivation and effect is legitimacy, that is, to become and be recognized as more like others in the field.

Limits to public purposes of private schools

An example of institutional isomorphism in private education that has a direct relationship to the theme of this book is the charitable status of private schools in the United Kingdom. Private or privately funded schools are in some important ways distanced from state control more than their state sector alternatives. In their comparison of quasi-markets of schooling in nineteen countries Lubienski and Linick (2011) argued that non-state schools in England and Wales received comparatively a low level of state funding, and are subjected to a low level of regulation. More recently there has been debate in policy circles about increasing state expectations and regulation of private schools (e.g. BBC, 2014; Hunt, 2014). In England privately funded schools are released from delivering the national curriculum that government maintained schools teach and have greater flexibility in curriculum than state-funded privately governed academy schools; academies are not bound by the national curriculum but they must teach a core of English, mathematics and science and religious education, whereas there is no core for fee-paying private schools. Yet privately funded schools are not entirely deregulated in respect of curriculum. They must provide a curriculum that includes 'linguistic, mathematical, scientific, technological, human and social, physical and aesthetic and creative education' (Schedule to the Education (Independent School Standards) Regulations 2014), and provision for the 'spiritual, moral, social and cultural development of pupils' that 'actively promotes the fundamental British values of democracy, the rule of law, individual liberty, and mutual respect and tolerance of those with different faiths and beliefs', and precludes 'the promotion of partisan political views', offering a balanced view of political issues if they arise. Schools are also required to undergo inspection by a government-approved inspection agency, although for privately funded schools this is not restricted to Ofsted (a non-ministerial government department) as is the case with state-funded schools. Their governance arrangements are also more flexible than other schools. It is a requirement that the school is led by a proprietor who the earlier 2010 Independent School Standards defined as 'the person or body of persons responsible for the management of the school and includes individual proprietors or formally constituted boards of governors, directors or trustees'. The Standards currently refer to a proprietor as either an individual or 'a body of persons corporate or unincorporated'. Privately funded private schools may be either profit-generating businesses (sole traded or limited companies) or charitable companies; this is unlike academies which currently are all exempt charitable trusts. The business structures of the schools determine the nature of the proprietor.

Privately funded schools are regulated to an extent in their educational purpose and curriculum under education law and also are subject to legislation in other areas such as equalities, companies and, when they have charitable status, charity law. However, the extent and intensity of government regulation is not evenly distributed between different kinds of governance structure or across fields of law. In the United Kingdom, most privately funded schools are charities rather than profit-making entities, although according to recent Independent School Council figures the number of charities in this sector is in decline. In 2013, 82 per cent of their member schools were charities, but in 2018 this had declined to 75 per cent (ISC, 2013; 2018). Charity status has conferred the advantage of tax concessions (Fairburn, 2013), although this advantage is under scrutiny in England and Wales, and subject to reform in Scotland. Schools with charitable status are subject to charity law; however, charity law covers a vast array of activities with multiple purposes and consequently can be quite ambiguous about its strictures. Charity law means that private schools must adhere to one or more of the purposes of charities (of which one is the advancement of education) and additionally contribute to public benefit. Yet charity law does not comprehensively define public benefit, and its meaning and assumptions can only be derived from pre-existing cases. As a result, there has been considerable debate over the meaning of public benefit and how it can be achieved through the advancement of education (Millar, 2011; Fairburn, 2013). Yet even without clear guidance on what counts as public benefit private schools that adopt charitable status have tended to interpret it in similar kinds of ways, in particular offering bursaries to students who could not otherwise attend and making school facilities available to local communities and state-funded schools. In England and Wales this commonality between approaches was evident even prior to 2008, which is before the Charity Commission initiated public benefit assessments that proved to be controversial and were the basis of legal challenge.

With public benefit assessment the Charity Commission sought to develop case studies of public benefit to provide examples of good practice and show why some charities were deemed not to have met public benefit requirements. The Charity Commission reported on twelve cases, of which five were private schools. Three of these schools were judged to have met the criterion of public benefit, demonstrating some level of convergence in their practices towards public benefit, whereas two were not. The head teacher of one of the schools that failed the assessment was reported in the *Times* as saying:

> As a stand-alone prep school, we just don't have the pot that other schools have. We failed only because we're not producing enough bursaries. But nowhere in

> the course of this process has the commission given us a clear idea of what we need to achieve. It's like being told you've failed a maths exam but without being told what the passmark is. (Northcott, 2009 cited in Fairburn, 2013, p. 22)

However, the Charity Commission produced guidance throughout 2008, including *Charities and Public Benefit* (January 2008), *Public Benefit and Fee-Charging* and *The Advancement of Education for the Public Benefit* (both published in December 2008). These publications became the target of legal challenge initiated by the Independent Schools' Council. The Tribunal that presided over the judicial review of the Charity Commission's guidance on public benefit proposed quashing the whole of *Public Benefit and Fee-Charging* and parts of the other two publications, which forced the Charity Commission to withdraw the former publication and make amendments to the latter two. The remaining guidance remains vague and continues to rely heavily on case law or exemplars in the interpretation of what counts as public benefit. While their aim is to assess individual circumstances, the cases have a significant structuring influence on the way schools ensure they meet requirements. By 2010 the Charity Commission reported that the two schools that had failed the public benefit assessment had now developed strategies to address their concerns. S. Anselm's School has since added to its activities in the Charity register that it opens 'the school facilities for the benefit of the local community', and Highfield Priory School reported in 2017 on its provision of bursaries and sharing of facilities with community groups. The examples they cite are from just two of around 1,300 schools that are charities, which raises the concern that their practices will take on inordinate significance as examples of public benefit.

In 2013 a report by the UK government's Public Administration Select Committee (PASC) suggested that the Charity Commission is asked to do too much and not sufficiently resourced to ensure public benefit from organizations awarded charitable status. They also reported that contributing to limits on the Charity Commission's resource and role as regulator was its need to defend itself and take a leading role in the legal proceedings related to the definition of public benefit.

> The legal disputes relating to the Charity Commission's interpretation of "public benefit" and the Charities Act 2006 are complex and touch upon controversial and political questions concerning charitable status. This has also been a considerable financial burden on the Charity Commission and on the charities concerned, which is itself an injustice. (PASC, 2013, p. 54)

So, there is no statutory definition of public benefit in England and Wales charity law, the Charity Commission guidelines on public benefit for private schools are contested and the Charity Commission lacks the time and resources to do more than a modicum of regulation of private schools. As schools move further away from government regulation, they are apparently free to innovate, yet despite loose regulation from the Charity Commission private schools provide public benefit in remarkably similar ways. While many schools were already converging around similar practices, the public debate and legal challenge has largely worked to further structure the field and embed existing practice. Non-conforming schools gain their legitimacy through coercion and are forced into line with the examples of schools that have demonstrable public benefit, and any innovation from current practice runs the risk of being outside of the broad and ill-defined parameters of public benefit. That there are limitations to publicness within private education is not a revelation. Yet even an association between public benefit and private schools is an interesting problematic that raises the possibility of the recontextualization of private school policy through democratic and expansive pedagogic discourse.

Conditional publicness in English private schools

The history of private education and its debates between public and private education provide important insight on the possible public dimensions of private education. Cohen (2004) returns to the eighteenth-century enlightenment debate on public versus private education as a means to understand not only how differences in meaning between public and private have developed but also how intrinsically they are in their different manifestations related to conceptualizations of gender. She starts her argument with the clear distinction English philosopher John Locke contributed to the debate between private and public education in his 1693 work *Some Thoughts Concerning Education*. Private education he distinctly associated with education in the home, whereas public education was education in the school. At this point ideas about providing free and compulsory schooling funded by the state had started to permeate Europe and had been translated into practice in the state of Weimar in 1619, but was a long way from being legislated in England (Ramirez and Boli, 1987). However, there existed large grammar and other public schools that were generally free to attend, funded by endowments or charity. Very few children did attend, and the oft repeated justification is that few could afford time away from their own and their family's subsistence; however, inequalities in cultural capital and its enactment through informal impediments such as use of protocols and continuance of family traditions must also have worked to limit their intake. Locke's work referred to these schools, and his argument was that they were inferior to private education within the home where virtues could be cultivated. The story of public schooling is associated with the expansion of the middle class throughout the eighteenth century, when the grammar and great schools disparaged by Locke became increasingly popular and proliferated. These schools were public, therefore, in that they operated outside of the domestic sphere. The point made by Cohen (2004) is that the expansion of schooling in response to the rise in the middle classes also led to clearer definition and separation in education of the sexes, as public schooling came to be associated with masculinity, and femininity associated with the private education acquired in the home. The social mores of the times dictated that in general boys attended school, and girls if they were educated at all were educated at home. Even though fee paying started much earlier, separation between public and private schooling on financial grounds was a later phenomenon of nineteenth-century education policy reform. This included the Public Schools Act 1868, which set apart from public agencies seven of the great or most elite fee-paying public schools (Eton, Winchester, Westminster, Charterhouse, Harrow, Rugby and Shrewsbury) under their own boards of governance, and the education reform acts between 1870 and 1893 that established compulsory fee-free state education in England and Wales.

The confusing term public school came to be used in common language to define other privately funded schools in the United Kingdom, and it has only been in recent times the terminology has generally shifted to independent schools, often by those who support them, or private schools by those who do not. Yet a number still retain at least informally the status of 'public school' through their membership of the Headmasters' and Headmistresses' Conference (HMC), an association of what the HMC claims are the world's leading schools. In the eighteenth century public schools' association with the public sphere was based in their point of difference from the closed realm of the home. As their nomenclature has shifted towards private school, their association with closure is their restricted access, that is, access is restricted by the ability to pay school fees (Benn and Downs, 2015). Yet there seems to remain an association between the private of private education and gender. Statistics for private schools in England suggest that only slightly more boys than girls enrol in the sector overall, yet in the HMC public schools only 35 per cent of students are girls. While HMC schools are undoubtedly not public education in any common-sense usage of the term, they confer positional advantage out in the world and well beyond the restrictions of the domestic sphere. Their influence is global. According to the facts and figures HMC supplies on their website, 'over the past 15 years HMC schools in England have opened 21 overseas campuses which, between them, educate more than 15,000 pupils'.

Many others have examined the segregating effects of elite education and its relationship to cultural and economic capital (Koh and Kenway, 2016; Koinzer et al., 2017), and it is not the purpose of this book to either re-examine in-depth these social relations or justify them in the service of its reconceptualization of publics. Indeed, the opposite of the latter is truer. Recognition of social segregation is an important element in understanding the limits or conditions placed upon publics and pluralist public entities. Segregation through schooling is an effect of power operating within and between fields of schooling. Within social field theory the field of power is like a meta-field that intersects with and regulates power relations in all other fields. Like other fields the organizational field of private schooling is affected not only by its own internal forces but also 'external forces that originate from within the field of power' (p. 191). Power struggles are played out between the cultural and economic fractions of the elite (Mangez and Hilgers, 2012), and these have evident effects within private schooling. Within private schooling as in other subfields of education there is 'an opposition between those who conceive education as an autonomous domain primarily concerned with cultural matters and those who emphasise education in relation to external concerns such as economic prosperity and competitiveness' (Mangez and Hilgers, 2012, p. 192). In Bourdieu's theorization of social structure cultural capital is subordinate to economic capital and for schools this means they are regulated by struggles between a dominated cultural elite and its values and a dominant economic elite. Cultural capital is valued within the field of private schooling for its capacity to serve the interests of economic capital; serving the interests of economic capital means the worth of private schooling is financial. From a financial perspective private schooling is a product that is consumed and like other products produced for consumption; its value increases through mass production or massification. In countries strongly committed to state-funded education, the massification of private schooling has not been to create vastly more privately funded schools but to introduce private interests to state-funded schooling, although interestingly the United Kingdom's private schools are exported to international markets. The private Repton School in Derbyshire, England, established an international arm that in 2019, according to its website, had three schools in the Middle East, one in Singapore and another four due to open soon.

Privatized education

In classical economics a public good is a commodity or benefit accessible to all members of a society with no exclusions as a result of non-payment or competition with another consumer. A private good provides benefit to people either as individual or groups while others are excluded from benefit. Herein we see the relationship established by Starr (1985) where public–private is conceptually linked with whole–part. Some of the positions in debates on public and private education put forward the view that education is a public good because its benefits are accessible to the whole of a society, and therefore education should be free to access and supported by the state. This view is particularly prevalent in debates on higher education (Nixon, 2010; Owen-Smith, 2018), where arguments are that even those not engaged directly in higher education benefit from the knowledge developed within universities or the education of others in their roles beyond the university. Yet governments' restricted funding of higher education and policies that support high fees, complex and burdensome student loan schemes and knowledge tied up in commercial activities exclude people from directly consuming its benefits. Underpinning such policies is the presumption that education is a private good. Privatization in education may be regarded as the shift from education perceived as a public good to education perceived as a private good (Ball and Youdell, 2008); yet, another common view is that education is integrally both a public and private good. As Levin (1999) explains:

> Education inherently serves both public and private interests (Levin, 1987). It addresses public interests by preparing the young to assume adult roles in which they can undertake civic responsibilities; embrace a common set of values; participate in a democratic polity with a given set of rules; and embrace the economic, political, and social life that constitute the foundation for the nation. All of this is necessary for an effectively functioning democracy, economy, and society. At the same time, education must address the private interests of students and their families by providing a variety of forms of development that will enhance individual economic, social, cultural, and political benefits for the individual. Embedded in the same educational experience are outcomes that can contribute to the overall society as well as those that can provide private gains to the individual. (Levin, 1999, p. 125)

Debates on whether education is a public or private good are important when grappling with ideas about educational privatization because they show how understandings of public and private are used to shape its social practices. That is, policy discourses of education as private or public good regulate practices that are called privatization, and shape experiences of education that might associate more with either the private or public. Yet the idea that education is a relation between a public and private good is perhaps the more useful concept for my argument. In Levin's conceptualization of education, education is represented self-evidently as a mixed good (Levin, 1999; Levin et al., 2013). This definition does not quite capture the fluidity of relations between the public and private in privatization, such as the hidden relations within positions that purport education to be wholly a private or public good. For me understanding privatization means recognizing that it represents an interrelationship between notions of the public and private, as well as that the bounded nature of concepts of public and private good only emerges through their use. Or from a policy perspective, that a broader public good of privatization than what may ever have been intended may be realized through the recontextualization of intended or actual policy as policy-in-use.

Privatization in many fields of the state sector has meant the sale of state-owned assets to private sector ownership, such as the telecommunications and energy sectors. Ball and Youdell (2008) called this exogenous privatization, where public services are opened up to ownership and management in the private sector. According to Ball and Youdell, in education exogenous privatization is a process of making public education private. Exogenous privatization is differentiated from endogenous privatization, the latter of which Ball and Youdell suggest is the introduction of private interests to public education. An example is the privatized schools, where the state retains ownership, but schools are privately managed and governed. While these two categories of privatization, exogenous and endogenous, has practicality because it describes what governments generally do in respect of privatization, its underpinning assumption is that public interests are associated with the state and private interests are associated with the market. As I have pointed out previously this distinction is exclusionary and obfuscating because it classifies all interests outside of the state as private or acts as a pre-legitimizing criterion for membership of a public, that is, through citizenship of a nation state. To follow earlier lines of argument the entities that emerge through educational privatization as defined by Ball and Youdell may exhibit characteristics of publicness. Privatization in education means some kind of relations between private and public interests, and while studies of privatization tend to emphasize the private aspect of these relations, as argued in the previous chapter in respect of public scrutiny of private interests we need also to maintain a line of sight to their publicness.

Privatization in some cases means a shift from state to private ownership of assets, yet accountabilities to the public good of such assets should exist in exogenous educational privatization whether the public is conceived as a mainstream public associated with the state or an alternative public. Some privatized educational entities have private ownership; there are shared ownership models through public–private partnerships; and then there are models of privatization where the state retains ownership, but other means of control are granted to private entities. In each case there is a blending of public and private interests that add layers of complexity to the forms of entity that develop. Making distinctions between different forms of ownership and funding arrangements may be helpful but only if they are sufficiently nuanced and are considered in conjunction with other practices of governance. Taking account of the variety of ownership models, regulatory frameworks, mission and who participates in decision-making provides a meaningful basis on which to distinguish different privatized entities when evaluating their public qualities. While different forms of governance and their complex relations between public and private interests are mapped out in the next chapter, here the purpose is to look more generally at conceptualizations of privatization and where we might find the public within them.

The privatization of the majority of educational state assets into fully private ownership is not common in the jurisdictions referred to in this book, perhaps reflecting the mixed interests inherent in their education systems. Countries where most of education is in private ownership tend not to have advanced development of compulsory or free schooling. Private ownership of schooling goes against the right to education as it is expressed through the work of the United Nations. The first of the Global Monitoring Reports (2002) for UNESCO's 2000 initiative Education for All (EFA) noted that in 1999, 91 per cent of countries had legislated for compulsory education; however, for many countries the extent of compulsory education was only to primary school level. A renewed commitment to state-funded education, free and compulsory for all children, was made by 180 countries in the Incheon Declaration of 2016:

> Motivated by our significant achievements in expanding access to education over the last 15 years, we will ensure the provision of 12 years of free, publicly funded, equitable quality primary and secondary education, of which at least nine years are compulsory. (p. 7)

While globally state-owned and state-funded education increases, this does not mean private interests in education have lessened. Indeed, the opposite is the case. As discussed in the previous section, some private entities have long existed prior to or alongside state-funded education. There are some privately owned entities that have emerged through forms of privatization in education, as the state has retreated from aspects of education. An example is the growth of privately owned educational services in England that have emerged as local authorities retreated from free and accessible service provision to schools, as a result of bulk funding cuts and redeployment of school budgets from the local authorities to new academy schools.

In their work on consultants and consultancy in education Gunter and Mills (2017) point to the establishment in the United Kingdom of the Society of Education Consultants in 1990 as a significant marker in the growth of the marketplace of educational services. They cite the organization's own description of its remit that claims members offer services to 'schools, LAs, HEIs, and other institutions' that are 'high quality, experienced professional help and support' (pp. 5–6). The year 1990 is significant because it was a period of educational policy reform by Conservative governments underpinned by market principles. The reforms included the introduction of parental choice to school admissions, compulsory parent representation on school boards of governors, linkage between enrolment numbers and funding, and opening the door to school league tables through the publication of school attainment data (Machin and Vignoles, 2006). Market-like conditions continued and expanded during the Labour governments of 1997–2010, but it was the election of a Liberal-Conservative coalition government in 2010 that raised the stakes. Many local authorities were already on the route towards privatization of educational services by 2010, but the Academies Act (2010) and bulk funding cuts as part of the programme of austerity were transformative in hastening the process. Local authorities in England 'lost 27 per cent of their spending power between 2010/11 and 2015/16 in real terms' (Hastings et al., 2015, p. 3), and the authorities most affected by funding cuts were in the quintile of authorities with the most deprived neighbourhoods according to the government's indices of deprivation. While these cuts affected public policy across all fields, academization worsened the financial loss for educational services because in addition to loss of core funding, money that had come to local authorities from school budgets was redistributed to individual or multi-academy trust boards. But for all public services the speed with which the cuts occurred meant that changes had to be implemented quickly without time to enact well-considered and sustainable change (ibid.).

Gunter and Mills (2017) identify four main types of changes that occur through the privatization of public services. The first are structural changes where the market is developed and expanded through the introduction of private providers and supporting industry, and privately owned services commissioned and regulated by the state. Second are changes related to the funding base with increasing contributions from private resources, perhaps families, charities or business sponsors, and the state purse allocated on formulas constructed along business lines such as voucher systems or demand from service users. Third are changes that reflect the priorities of private interests, such as the expansion of the school choice agenda and the individualization of service user need discussed in the previous chapter. Fourth and finally are the issues of concern that are relocated from the public sphere and therefore resourced as public services to be recast as the concerns of private individuals, communities or families and therefore less deserving of public resourcing. Each of these types of change was evident in my four case studies of privatization in local authorities. What interested me were the differences in ethos behind the changes in each of the four different sites (Boyask, 2015a). The local authorities were negotiating the shift from public to private by taking different stances on how far from the public they were willing to depart in respect of their issues of concern and what kinds of private interests they were willing to work with. Ultimately the intense financial pressure was such that they pushed the local authorities closer together than they would like in respect of their structure and funding bases, but within each of the four case study sites there was evidence of four different sets of values underpinning their interpretation of the public good and what they should do in the public interest. These differences I term community, co-operative, entrepreneurial and corporate privatization. While a more detailed analysis of these differences is undertaken in Chapter 7, evident even within the list of terms are quite different orientations to the role of public servants in local government. The community model of privatization sought to draw on the strength of its school community to overcome the shortfall in local government resources. The co-operative model sought to form partnerships of mutual benefit that were underpinned by co-operative values. The entrepreneurial model conceived of public servants as drivers of innovation. And, the corporate model was founded on a business partnership between a skeletal education services division within the local authority and a multinational corporation.

Within each of these models there existed privately owned entities, but there were also partnerships or shared ownership entities and fully state-owned entities, although the latter were under increasing pressure to restructure and reform as either partnership or private entities. For example, a senior manager in the co-operative local authority recognized that their internal school improvement service was no longer financially viable and told me that

> there are two main options that I've put on the table, and one is completely integrate our services with schools, and use the school community interest company framework as our framework and just move it. And the other one, as I've said to you, is some kind of joint venture company. (Interview, 3 April 2013)

Mentioned in this quote is a community interest company which is a new corporate legal structure that is designed with social rather than economic goals in mind. In the next chapter is discussed these and other kinds of corporate structure that might be employed in the service of different concepts of a public good. Also examined more closely is the notion of public–private partnerships and the complexities of bringing together public and private interests within a single entity.

Privatization in schooling

A discussion of privatization would be remiss if it also did not look in some detail at how privatization is enacted through education's most numerous and influential entities, schools. As indicated earlier in this chapter, schooling largely remains in state ownership despite the pervasive influences of market-driven ideology that values private ownership. Free and compulsory schooling remains a standard marker of a legitimate nation state evident through the 180 signatories to UNESCO's most recent EFA initiative. Since the last quarter of the twentieth century compulsory schooling policies have seen the introduction of private interests and a shift towards conceptualizing education as a private good. Concepts of the public have shifted since the earliest state-wide policies for free and compulsory public education, and consequently contemporary models of schooling reflect these changes. Private governance rather than private ownership is one of the main ways that privatization has taken root in modern-day compulsory schooling. This can be attributed to the desire to tap into the innovation and efficiency of the private sector, while retaining some state regulation and control for the purposes of equity (Lubienski, 2009).

State funding has conventionally been a feature of public education, yet schools such as academy schools in England, charter schools in the United States (which are gaining ground in the policy discourses emerging since the 2016 presidential election), free schools in Sweden, direct subsidy scheme schools in Hong Kong and independent public schools in Australia are privatized because these schools have control over their own budgets, and therefore may be regarded as in some respects autonomous from government. Some countries allow some or all of these state-funded schools to generate profit; others require that they remain non-profit bearing.

A report from the Organisation for Economic Co-operation and Development's (OECD) Programme for International Student Assessment (PISA), which compares national school systems, reviewed research evidence on the relationship between private versus public governance and social inequality (2012). The report suggests that while private governance offers opportunities for greater school choice and increases efficiency of schools, it also creates greater social stratification. They conclude that schools where there is public ownership but private governance may mitigate the problems of social inequality.

> Privately managed schools may have the authority to hire and compensate teachers and staff, and thus can select better-prepared teachers and introduce incentives for performance. Privately managed schools may also have more discretion on curricula and instructional methods, and so can adapt them to the interests and abilities of their students. (OECD, 2012, p. 9)

However, analysis of their own research findings by a number of researchers suggests that policies of public ownership and private governance need targeted approaches that direct resources towards disadvantaged students to overcome inequalities. They advocate for public accountability for self-governed schools in the spending of public money.

One of the most visible expressions of privatization (or retreat of the public) in England's schools has been the development of state-funded private schools through the academy schools programme. England has seen the growth of state-funded privately governed schooling through the academies programme, which has resulted in a new type of semi-autonomous school that is state funded and privately governed through an academy trust (which is a charitable company made up of two tiers of governance: members of the trust and the board of governors). The separation within academies between funding from the state and management through the academy trust means they adhere to the OECD's (2012) definition of a private school that is 'managed directly or indirectly by a non-government organisation' (p. 18).

The academy schools programme was originally a policy of the New Labour government that focused upon the improvement of 'under-performing' secondary schools in areas of high deprivation (DfEE, 2001). In 2002, three City Academies had opened, and by the end of the Labour government in 2010 the programme had expanded, but only with a target of 10 per cent of all state-funded secondary schools (Curtis et al., 2008). The succeeding Conservative/Liberal Democrat government was much more ambitious. On 26 May 2010, Michael Gove, secretary of state for education, invited all primary, secondary and special schools to apply for academy status 'offering them greater independence and freedom' (DfE, 2010a).

In mid-2013 there were 3,049 schools in the academy programme. These figures had risen from 130 academies in 2008 (Curtis et al., 2008). In England by March 2014, 54 per cent of all secondary schools and 11 per cent of all primary schools were academies according to government statistics.[1] A January release from the Department for Education indicated that in October 2018, 50.1 per cent of all pupils studying in state-funded schools were enrolled in an academy. Academy school status releases schools from most aspects of local government control and some aspects of central government control. Consequently, funding for these schools has been taken away from local authorities, who traditionally have had oversight of state-sector schooling and diverted to the schools themselves. Local authorities retain statutory responsibility for the performance of schools, yet almost all direct involvement with academies must be negotiated through optional service contracts (Boyask, 2013), and many academies opt to take their custom elsewhere. Among educationists there is considerable concern that privatized schools distanced from democratically elected government will not serve the public interest and will further entrench segregation and social inequality. In response to the policy for privatized schooling strong counter-discourses have emerged, for a return to democratic governance of schools (Hatcher, 2014) and the establishment of the common or comprehensive school (Fielding and Moss, 2010; Reay, 2012).

In England the Department for Education draws support for policy on autonomous schooling from the results of international comparative surveys like the OECD's PISA, and the International Association for the Evaluation of Educational Achievement (IEA) studies' Trends in International Mathematics and Science Study (TIMSS) and Progress in International Reading Literacy Study (PIRLS). Government ministers claim these studies prove that high achievement in the surveys is an outcome of educational policies that allow for greater school autonomy (Gove, 2012; Truss, 2013), even while OECD reports (2010; 2011b) on school autonomy suggest the relationship between student performance and school autonomy is very complex.

> At the country level, the greater the number of schools that have the responsibility to define and elaborate their curricula and assessments, the better the performance of the entire school system, even after accounting for national income ... .
>
> In contrast, there is no clear relationship between autonomy in resource allocation and performance at the country level. (OECD, 2011b, p. 2)

The support for school autonomy from government is accompanied by an accelerating programme of school reform that is exerting greater control on curriculum and assessment, and increasing schools' responsibility for resource allocation, resulting in the transformation of the schooling landscape, particularly within the secondary sector. Writing on reforms of the previous government in England, Simkins (1999) suggested that the neoliberal agenda within policy had resulted in the exercise of government power through both direct and indirect means. Even at this time, central government was constructing liberal policy that apparently allowed institutions to manage their own practices. Discourses of self-management obscured the reality that successful schools were either pressured into compliant behaviour through consumer demand, because schools now operated within a market-like environment, or government openly manipulated the performance of schools through inspection regimes and assessment targets.

In the first two chapters I raised the prospect of self-governing institutions contributing to an overall democratic order. Academy schools, particularly standalone academies with their self-governing boards, bear some similarities to the kinds of self-governing institutions Fraser (1990) may have been contemplating when she conceptualized counterpublic governance. Some groups have even sought to use the academies legislation to further social justice, such as establishing local curriculum (see Chapter 8). Yet academies also bear a resemblance to market entities and compete with one another for students and resources. The next chapter examines entities that are released from some elements of state control to pursue both economic and social interests. It considers the extent to which they are compelled to compromise or the extent to which they realize their public education ambitions.

Note

1 Figures were retrieved from the Department for Education EduBase2, Retrieved 27 March 2014, http://www.education.gov.uk/edubase (accessed 27 March 2014).

4

Mapping Governance Structures

In July 2013 Sir Christopher Kelly was charged with reviewing the circumstances that had led to a £1.5 billion capital shortfall in The Co-operative Bank of the United Kingdom and its subsequent near financial collapse. The report published the following year was entitled 'Failings in management and governance'. In his report, Kelly writes:

> I have been impressed during this review by the commitment and attachment shown by so many to the values and principles of the co-operative movement. That commitment makes more painful the failings in the Bank described in this report. (2014, p. 1)

The Kelly report and the media reports of the crisis at the bank before and after caught my attention because around this time there was a wave of optimism about the possibilities of co-operative schooling as a partial antidote to a competitive and market-driven schooling system (Coates, 2015; Mills, 2015). While there are considerable differences in purpose and practice between co-operative banks and co-operative schools, they both operate a governance structure that draws on the principles of the co-operative movement. Neither co-operative schools nor the Co-operative Bank operate in the ideal co-operative form of a consumer co-operative, owned and governed by members (with membership conferred through a membership scheme). Yet, reflection on the Co-operative Bank highlights that there are differences in governance structures informed by different sets of principles, and that some organizations actively adopt structures that reflect their commitment to the public good. It also highlights that ethical values such as equality, democracy and solidarity, three values from the co-operative movement that are identified in the ethical policy of the Co-operative Bank, must enter into some form of compromise to flourish in a competitive, market environment.

The financial crisis in The Co-operative Bank was also around the time I was investigating and writing about the challenges of enacting co-operative values in local government in England (Boyask, 2015a; 2018). I studied four local authorities close in proximity but differing considerably in ethos and demographics. It was a time of change in the local government sector that had a heavy impact on children's social and educational services. There were extensive cuts to central government's bulk funding to local authorities, who had traditionally acted as the caretakers of publicly funded schools, and further funding loss resulting from the Academies Act 2010 that shifted school funding away from local authorities and redirected it to individual and groups of schools. One of the local authorities studied was a co-operative Council that claimed it worked from co-operative values, defined by the Council as democracy, responsibility, fairness and partnership. These values did not feature overtly in my research data. Yet, there were important ways that the decisions the Council made connected with co-operative values, such as a commitment to partnership with local school leader groups and discussions with them on establishing a co-operative or mutual organization to develop strategies for school improvement. Co-operative values made more significant inroads into education with a co-operative version of every type of school emerging in England's fragmenting school system (Courtney, 2015). Paradoxically while co-operative schools emerge from the co-operative movement they do not run as consumer co-operatives, owned and run by their members (Woodin, 2014). Frameworks applicable to the type of school they adopt regulate them (Coates, 2015; Mills, 2015). What they have in common with co-operatives and one another are the values and principles of the co-operative movement in their conceptualization and practice (Woodin, 2014). Co-operative schools enact co-operative principles by developing a governance structure that involves members of the organization in decisions around teaching, learning and governance (Woodin, 2014). The co-operative principle of democratic or public participation of members in decisions that affect them is what qualifies these schools for inclusion in this book. Woodin describes co-operative schools as hybrid or embryonic co-operatives, but I think a more helpful term is conditional co-operatives. They have adapted to their circumstances or conditions; the laws that regulate the forms they adopt act to constrain their co-operativeness, and therefore publicness, yet there is always some space for variation in form. However, the compromises on co-operative values that some schools make when adapting to the prevailing conditions can be large (Dennis, 2017).

Obviously, co-operative schools differ from banking in that where the Co-operative Bank was a solution for doing private finance more ethically, co-operative schools are attempting to do public education more ethically.

'Public education' is a powerful symbol of desire that is shaped by a sense of loss and nostalgia for a non-existent past that stands in contrast to the intrusion of the market in education (Gerrard, 2015). In this imaginary of public education schools are established on ideals of social unity and equality and detached from the values of market exchange. Yet the common school of public education is not entirely distinct from the world of business. For Dewey (1915) the common school that had materialized through industrialization demanded weakened boundaries between school and industry, and he advocated for curriculum built upon the occupations of citizens beyond the walls of the school.

> But in the school the typical occupations followed are freed from all economic stress. The aim is not the economic value of the products, but the development of social power and insight. It is this liberation from narrow utilities, this openness to the possibilities of the human spirit, that makes these practical activities in the school allies of art and centers of science and history. (Dewey, 1915, p. 16)

Contemporary schools drawing from the co-operative and mutual movement, which is grounded in business practice, is consistent with a tradition of common schooling as an embryonic society and where 'occupations are made the articulating centers of school life' (p. 12). It differs because while they share co-operative values, the co-operative movement is an economic movement. Yet contemporary co-operative schools are grappling with an entanglement between the values of public education and those of economics. The economic stress they face is not just in respect of preparing children to be economically productive through their systems of curriculum and assessment but also governance, management, acquisition and allocation of resources. The solution to mitigating economic stress of the co-operative movement is to take ownership of the means of production and collectively govern these means for the benefit of all involved. There are other ways that schools and other educational organizations manage economic stress, such as by adopting conventional business models or some of the more recent and diverse types of legal entity developed in response to greater intermeshing of social and economic interests in public life.

This chapter identifies and maps entities that support the intermeshing of educational and economic interests. It is concerned foremost with the types of entities used in education to maintain a commitment to the values of public education, even while they are forced into compromise with values of the market. It focuses specifically on the structures these entities adopt, including their legal forms, ownership models, the regulatory fields in which they operate, and considers the extent to which they can be classified as public entities. The entities discussed attempt to moderate the effects of market competition through adopting governance structures that engage with concepts of the public, yet not public in a common-sense definition of the public where public is synonymous with the state or an abstract totality like the general public. Public is understood in relation to an all-subjected principle, whereby the public exists only as it is subjected to structures of governance (Abizadeh, 2012), and structures such as the public entities examined are conceptualized as pluralist, contextually specific, discursive and partial (Fraser, 1990; Warner, 2002). These publics are conditional, because even while they pursue the public good through social goals, mutual human relations or environmental ethics, they are shaped by an economic imperative as either an explicit or implicit goal.

Struggle for the public in conditional public entities

There is an expansive literature on new relationships between public and private interests and their myriad of forms, such as public–private partnerships (PPPs) (Robertson et al., 2012), edu-businesses as providers of education, consultancy and accreditation (Thompson et al., 2016; Gunter et al., 2015) and state-funded privately governed education institutions (Wells et al., 2002; Trimmer, 2013). Research in this area focuses on the extent to which the involvement of business or private interests erodes public education in both its form and intent. Less common is scholarship that attempts to step aside from the main critiques of market models of education to consider whether nuances in market-like relations, such as Yeatman (2007) on a refined understanding of the individual in individualism, Blackmore (2016) on the use of social justice principles in educational administration and leadership or Dennis (2017) on co-operative schools as an ethical alternative to academization, can mitigate the worst aspects of educational markets. My own research in this area has focused upon examining and evaluating the public dimensions in the governance of fully private or privatized educational entities (Boyask, 2015a; 2015c; 2018).

The public in this chapter is shaped by debates in political and cultural theory about the nature and extent of the public, particularly the democratic public, in notions such as public good, public benefit and, specifically, public education. As outlined in Chapter 2 the position adopted on the nature of the public follows and extends from Abizadeh's (2012) notion of an unbounded people. Abizadeh argues that the demos, or democratic public, is defined by a principle of subjection. That is, political power is legitimized to all those subjected by it, but he abandons the argument that subjection is legitimized pre-politically to identifiable groups. In political theory the efficacy of a democracy is tied to the legitimacy and constitution of its public. Who legitimately participates in opinion formation and decision-making? A nation state delineates the boundaries of its public through rights to citizenship, yet many modern democrats point out that national laws have influence on more than just citizens. Legitimacy drawn in reference to an all-affected principle (i.e. a public is constituted through self-organization of groups in response to the human actions that affect them (Karlsson, 2006)) produces fickle boundaries that need to be drawn and redrawn, raising questions of who is legitimately empowered to draw them. Pre-legitimizing criteria like nationality, ethnicity or other forms of group membership such as in the cases of local publics examined in this chapter act to exclude some interests and privilege others, undermining the democratic principles of social justice and equality. Fraser (2010; 2014) argues that an all-subjected principle provides more stable and inclusive governance. That is, political power is legitimized to all those subjected by it. However, an all-subjected principle may not solve the problem of exclusion through boundaries either, since it 'presumes that the relevant community is already determined and that there is already a state in place to maintain the laws and do the subjecting' (Karlsson, 2006, p. 24). Abizadeh argues that the demos, or democratic public, is defined by a principle of subjection but applies it to a notion of an unbounded people. The limits of the people are established through the practice of self-rule, 'bounded only by the capacity of communicative decision-making practices to track the outward extended reach of political power' (Abizadeh, 2012, p. 881). This position takes us beyond asking 'who is the public', who in principle cannot be defined as a bounded group other than through practice. Instead we can focus upon practices from which publics are constructed and the conditions under which they exist.

The types of entities mapped here are used in education to maintain a commitment to the values of public education, even while they are forced into compromise with values of the market. What are the structures these entities adopt, that is, what are their legal forms, ownership models and the regulatory fields in which they operate? And to what extent do these structures contribute to their publicness or actively work against it?

The entities already introduced in earlier chapters attempt to moderate the effects of market competition through adopting governance structures that engage with concepts of the public. Public in this book is understood in relation to an all-subjected principle, whereby the public exists only as it is subjected to structures of governance (Abizadeh, 2012), and structures such as the public entities outlined in this chapter below are conceptualized as pluralist, contextually specific, discursive and partial (Fraser, 1990; Warner, 2002). Warner's (2002) definition of the public recognizes the unbounded and self-organizing principles of publics. Circulating discourses form and reform publics, creating relations between individuals and entities where previously there may have been none. Understanding public education from this perspective requires paying close attention to its enactment, that is, how its ideals are translated, voiced, interpreted and recontextualized through discourse and practice within prevailing socio-political conditions. The implication of an unbounded public for understanding public education is that the focus shifts from categorizing some institutions as public and others as private to recognizing publicness (in the sense of the practice of being public) in different types of institutions, even those that might ordinarily be regarded as private. The latter position is the one that underpins this chapter, initially in recognition that neither how we commonly understand public education in contemporary democracies, that is, education funded by the state, nor in its ideal form as education free to access, common to all and based on the values needed by a democratic citizenry, are sufficient for describing public education transformed through the neoliberal erosion of democracy. More recently I have argued that there remains even within privatized institutions a concept of publicness. Privatization changes public education, bringing with it the risks of the marketplace which is a competitive environment of winners and losers. Yet there are differences in approaches to privatization, with some driven by public interests rather than profit making (Boyask, 2015a).

Kelly moderated his views on The Co-operative Bank's financial failure by stating that the incompetence in management and governance was not indicative of failures of co-operative models of governance generally, and that there are qualitative differences between types of co-operative governance structure. However, publication of the review made the tensions between market competition and co-operative governance painfully obvious, because the internal failings of governance were front-page news and subtleties like the type of co-operative governance structure were lost in the following headlines:

Review castigates Co-op Bank management and board. (*Financial Times*, 1 May 2014)

Co-op Bank report hits out at poor management and overambition. (*The Guardian*, 30 April 2014)

Damning report blasts Co-operative Bank executives. (*Manchester Evening News*, 30 April 2014)

At the time of writing The Co-operative Bank continues to struggle, with a final severance from the Co-operative Group (one of the world's largest consumer co-operatives) in September 2017, and further branch closures announced in January 2018. The underlying dynamic between cooperation and competition can result in catastrophic failures and major social upheaval, as will be the case if the bank finally fails. More commonly, this dynamic sits in unresolved tension where small battles play out and are won or lost. However, Kelly's report makes a statement about differences between types of governance structure that is important to a discussion on public education within a neoliberal state. Kelly writes:

> My comments on governance should not be interpreted as a criticism of the co-operative model or of co-operative principles and values, for which I have a great deal of respect. It is the particular method of governance adopted by the Co-operative Group and Bank which in my view has manifestly failed, not the co-operative ideal in general. The current governance structure in the Co-operative Group, which dates only from 2001, is not the only way of putting co-operative principles into practice. (2014, p. 1)

Is it the case that some kinds of governance structure can mitigate the worst aspects of educational markets? Are there some resilient enough to resist competitive relations and minimize their impact on the public good? Should proponents of public education pay greater attention to governance type? The development of co-operative schools of different type suggested that it is less important for schools to be of a type (charitable trust school, academy school, free school, for example) than operate from an ethos. Yet research in various sites and across the years suggests that wider discursive and regulatory fields affect the capacity of institutions that intend to work for the public good to fulfil their ambitions (Boyask, 2015c; Mills, 2015). Hence it is difficult to enact co-operative values in the interactions between local government and schools, and between schools with one another when they are operating in a wider environment of competition for students, positional prestige (i.e. high placement in a league table) and funding. Yet desire to enact co-operative values through schooling is testament to hope for more fairness and equality in education. Dennis (2017) suggests that the hope lies in the translation of co-operative ideals to co-operative practice. The practice of governance is of especial importance to translating ideals into practice, because it establishes the context in which decision-making occurs, defines who participates in decision-making and what informs decisions.

The remainder of this chapter examines the practice of governance through the legal and conceptual models and entities that have in recent years developed, been used or rejected to engage with the public good of education, recognizing where they come into conflict or compromise with private or economic interests. It also highlights the expansion and development of new types of entity that enmesh public education purposes and private interests.

Corporations: For the benefit of members?

Educational organizations that take the form of businesses are subject to corporate law. That there is significance to the public good in differences between types of corporate entity initially occurred to me when reflecting upon data from my study of local authorities. One of the local authorities in the study had consciously adopted a fully marketized approach to services to schools (i.e. administrative, managerial and pedagogical support). Its response to funding cuts was to reduce its core services to a minimum and outsource all other services predominantly from the company it established. The Council retained a 20 per cent stake in its service company, a limited liability partnership, with the remaining 80 per cent held by a subsidiary of a FTSE 250 index listed company whose other areas of operation include training for the defence sector, engineering for the nuclear industry and construction of military aircraft. School leaders surveyed from the region were disparaging of the Council's decision to take public funds from central government and schools and deliver them into the hands of a profit-making entity (Boyask, 2018). The connection between the company and the defence industry was also heavily criticized, with one school leader disparaging of the local authority's partnership with 'an arms dealer'. Putting aside the ethics of mixing children's schooling with military defence, there are entrenched incompatibilities between the missions and responsibilities of these two different entities.

The public authority is wholly responsible for upholding the public good in respect of children and their education, which at the time was conceived very narrowly but still included:

- Ensuring a sufficient supply of school places
- Tackling underperformance in schools and ensuring high standards
- Supporting vulnerable children (Parish et al., 2012)

A public company is mostly responsible to the individuals who have invested funds in the business, and ensuring it returns to them a profit. A public company, like private companies, exists to benefit investors or shareholders and minimize its liability to others. The adoption of a limited liability company structure limits the responsibility of individual beneficiaries for a company's failings. It is of note that the education services limited liability partnership lists no individuals as members, only the Council and a private limited liability corporation, in its document of incorporation (i.e. document of formation as a corporation). This example sits in stark contrast to, at least to the intentions of, the co-operative Council in the same study.

The co-operative Council had responded differently to its reduction in finances. It cut services but opted to retain as many as possible, responding to the changed financial environment by offering them to schools as traded services. They produced a directory of services to schools that identified core services to schools still maintained by the local authority and offered traded services (individual pay-as-you-use or packages) to schools that received their own funding or wanted services not covered by the core agreement. However, the head of services recognized that the challenging financial circumstances for the local authority and schools meant the scheme was not sustainable and that further restructuring was required. They were investigating developing a partnership with local school leaders who had set up their own organizations for both primary and secondary schools to support each other with professional development and sharing expertise. The schools struggled to work co-operatively. The locality suffered from extreme competition because despite falling school roll numbers the central government had permitted the development of five new schools through its policies for school diversification. Existing schools were struggling to attract sufficient numbers of students, especially at the secondary school level. A senior manager at the local authority suggested the relations between schools were combative, and that an important element of the local authority's role was to help schools work together (even those who had opted to cut loose from the local authority). She also suggested that they were considering using a co-operative or mutual structure for the company they planned to develop, thus involving its members in governance.

Mutual and co-operative structures have a long history in business and industry, with some claiming their origins predate industrialization. However, their emergence is generally associated with the industrial revolution in England, and they are theoretically linked to liberalist views of self-dependence (Patmore and Balnave, 2018). In contemporary times their legal structure varies from one jurisdiction to another, but essentially either a mutual or co-operative serves the interests of its customers or members, and membership bestows governance or control rights over the organization. In Canada and the United States the mutual structure is largely relegated to insurance companies, where the beneficiaries become beneficiaries by virtue of holding an insurance policy with the company. This differs slightly from a true co-operative structure. Members or service users own a stake in a consumer co-operative through a membership scheme of some type, not from purchasing a service. A more important distinction is the difference between a mutual or co-operative ownership structure and its legal form. There are government Acts that specifically regulate co-operatives and give them legal form, such as the Co-operative Companies Act 1996 in New Zealand and Canada Co-operatives Act 1998. In the United Kingdom, there are two specific types of legal structure that are essentially mutual – Co-operative Societies and Community Benefit Societies regulated through the Co-operative and Community Benefit Societies Act 2014. Co-operative Societies benefit members who share a set of interests. Community Benefit Societies benefit a wider social group. Co-operatives in the UK, however, are not necessarily Co-operative Societies and many of them opt to take on the legal form of a limited liability company. This is because theoretically a limited liability company can be owned by, governed by and benefit its investors. This was the case with The Co-operative Bank, which is a public limited company; however, since the restructuring and recapitalization programme introduced in 2013 to resolve its financial difficulties its governance structure has moved further away from the co-operative ownership model and severed its formal links with The Co-operative Group. The bank retains its name on agreement with the co-operative sector body, Co-operative UK, because it claims it continues to uphold the co-operative values in its Articles of Association and its ethical policy (self-help, self-responsibility, democracy, equity and solidarity, equality). The extent to which these values are enacted is outside the scope of this book.

In schooling, the field is more complex, because even though many state-funded schools have come to operate more like businesses or gone into partnership with businesses, they are regulated by education legislation, and sometimes exempt from the requirements placed on other organizations of a similar legal type. Schools often are regarded as entities for the public benefit so will be discussed in more detail in the following section, but there are some schools that operate fully as co-operatives and therefore are private schools owned and run by their members. These schools claim to operate on co-operative principles such as democracy and equality, yet these values are limited to members not just because they are private schools but also because that is how consumer co-operatives work. Co-operative schooling has gained respect and credibility among educators looking for greater equality in education, but it is important to recognize what it is and what it is not. Mutual relations and participation in a co-operative are limited to those similarly positioned as a member of the group. It does not extend to social groups other than your own, which is a qualification of democracy in education at least in Deweyan terms. John Dewey's (1916) democratic ideal includes the extent to which members have 'an equable opportunity to receive and to take from others' and a 'large variety of shared undertakings and experiences' (p. 92). It also includes 'freer interaction between social groups' and 'change in social habit – its continuous readjustment through meeting the new situations produced by varied intercourse' as different social groups interact (p. 94). The co-operative ideal has the characteristics of a bounded public, a quantifiable social group that acts as a public yet is restricted by its pre-legitimizing criteria.

Charitable, not-for-profit and public benefit organizations

There are many organizations where the primary purpose extends beyond its members. The kinds of organizations of interest here are the organizations that have a social or public benefit. Schools generally fall into this category, as they offer a public service although there may be important differences depending upon where funding comes from. Public benefit is a topic analysed and discussed in depth in Chapter 5, in particular the tensions that emerge around the production of profit. In New Zealand legal entities required to report to the government for financial purposes must disclose whether they are profit orientated or public benefit entities (External Reporting Board, 2015). This disclosure distinguishes legal entities from one another before even considering whether they are charities, companies or Crown Entities (Crown Entities are a legal form in New Zealand for entities such as schools where the government has a controlling interest, yet from which they are legally separate). There is a further distinction in the New Zealand conceptual framework for public benefit entities between public sector public benefit entities (i.e. entities that deliver services to the general public) and not-for-profit public benefit entities (i.e. entities providing 'goods or services for community or social benefit rather than for a financial return to equity holders' (ibid., p. 7, ¶24.1)). However, since 2010 at least thirty states in America have passed legislation permitting for-profit public benefit corporations (PBCs) (Glover et al., 2016). While the legislation varies from one state to another, the common characteristic is that their activities fulfil their commitment to public benefit, outlined in their governing documents, as well as provide a financial return to stakeholders. The pursuit of profit makes PBCs significantly different from other public benefit entities, so these are examined in a later section alongside social enterprise. The New Zealand conceptualization of a public benefit entity differentiates it from a profit-making entity, with expectation that in a public benefit entity profit is not a motivating factor and profits are returned to the public beneficiaries through extending the entity's public service.

The Community Benefit Societies of the United Kingdom, mentioned earlier, are similarly a type of entity that benefits a group wider than its members and can be set up to benefit the public generally. In the latter case, where the public generally rather than a closed group benefits, the entity can qualify for charitable status, indeed, a legal form that lends itself to charitable purposes. Charitable purposes vary between jurisdictions, reflecting their own legislative priorities. For example, Australia recognizes 'promoting reconciliation' as a charitable purpose in its charity law (Charities Act 2013 (Cth)) in consideration of the impact of its colonial history on its indigenous peoples. In the Charities Act 2011 of England and Wales, the 'prevention or relief of poverty' is the first of its thirteen listed charitable purposes. Charity law in New Zealand, Australia and the United Kingdom all identify public benefit as an essential characteristic of charitable status. The public who benefits is defined in New Zealand law as 'the general public or a sufficient section of the community' (Charities Services, n.d.), and the main consideration for assessment is who can benefit. While in some circumstances limiting direct beneficiaries may be justifiable such as towards members of the public with a particular disability, a charity must prove wider public benefits in attending to the needs of a particular subsection of society.

Charitable purpose and charity law is particularly important for education in the United Kingdom, where many schools have charitable status. Most private schools opt for charitable status. In both England and Wales there are types of state-funded schools classified as exempt schools (foundation and trust schools, voluntary aided or controlled schools), or exclusively in England Academy schools. Exemption means they are exempted from reporting on their charitable purpose, since they are presumed to automatically be of public benefit. Exempt status is accorded to schools because they are assumed to be non-selective, with an open admissions process. This is in contrast to the selective entry of grammar schools that are the only schools permitted to select students based on high ability, usually determined through the results of an entrance test. All English schools have admissions criteria, set either by the school or its local authority, and select students on that basis. The School Admissions Code that schools must follow when setting their criteria with the force of law, allows for various selection processes in partially selective or, even what are usually considered to be, non-selective schools. Partially selective schools might opt to select up to 10 per cent of students in a specialist subject area like art or sport, or some admission authorities permit selection to fulfil a quota for ability bands within a school. Non-selective schools are required to accept all students within their catchment areas, unless they are oversubscribed in which case they should apply selection criteria compliant with the Admissions Code and any relevant legislation, including equalities legislation. In practice, even non-selective schools sometimes manipulate intake, including requesting prohibited information in admissions applications (West et al., Hind, 2011). Private schools that are charities are not exempt from reporting on their charitable purpose, and there are many organizations other than schools that have an educative role and are charities and therefore required to report on public benefit.

Charities in the United Kingdom can opt for a range of legal forms, and most take the form of an unincorporated association, company, trust or the relatively new legal form of the charitable incorporated organization (CIO). The majority of charities are companies, and CIOs have developed to reduce the amount of reporting for a charity with substantial business responsibilities. Private schools that are charities tend to take a company form, and state-funded schools tend to be charitable trusts. Charities establish their charitable purpose and plans for public benefit in their instruments of government, and report on their performance annually to the Charity Commission of England and Wales, Scottish Charity Regulator or The Charity Commission for Northern Ireland. Private schools are not deemed to be of public benefit automatically, because their benefits are usually restricted to those who can afford to attend. Charitable status requires that they set out aims for public benefit in their governing documents. Rugby School, a well-known privately governed and funded independent school, has activities in the following areas to demonstrate its commitment to public benefit: scholarships and bursaries, financial support for local schools, community partnerships and curriculum development and impact on national developments in education (Rugby School, 2014). There is considerable controversy about the charitable status of private schools, and recently Scotland, which like Northern Ireland has a charities regulator separate from the one in England and Wales, has reformed benefits private schools receive from their status as charities. In Scotland from 2020 private schools' eligibility for charity property rates relief will be revoked, and they will be required to pay full business rates (Scottish Government, 2017). Charities receive significant tax reliefs for public benefit and yet there are questions raised on the extent to which their work contributes to the public good.

Public–private partnerships

There is an extensive literature on PPPs, in recognition of their spread through globalization and the global dispersal of neoliberal policies. There are advocates for their use in the delivery of public services. There are many critics of their use. It is not the work of this book to recount the full body of work in this area. Nor does it take the position of Davies and Hentschke (2006) who aimed to study PPPs as politically neutral and objective researchers, staying clear of the controversy surrounding the relations between government and private sector interests. The controversy is what makes this form of governance interesting to my investigation because it highlights gaps between the aspirations for and the reality of PPPs, and therefore the compromises to public interests made by PPPs.

Discussing the role of PPPs in education governance, Robertson, Mundy, Verger and Menashy (2012) suggest PPPs are an arrangement of cooperation between institutions in the public and private sectors or, more particularly, their cooperation on the development and delivery of services and products, and the sharing of risks, resources and costs associated with them. The arrangements between partners vary, for example, in respect of the financial arrangements and nature of their relationships. Hodge and Greve (2007) presented a typology of PPPs based on the nature of the relationships between partners, that is, a matrix of tight or loose financial and organizational relationships. Tight financial and organizational relationships may be expressed through joint-venture companies, such as those proposed or enacted by local authorities in their services to schools in the discussions above. Other examples of PPPs in education that involve public expenditure include the Private Finance Initiatives (PFIs), which in the typology are founded on tight financial and loose organizational relationships, and are used to fund capital projects in education, particularly real estate such as school buildings. The financial arrangements in a PFI mean that the private investor usually covers up-front costs and manages the project, while the public partner leases back the utility and sometimes pays additional maintenance costs. An example of a high-profile PFI type of arrangement in education was the Building

Schools for the Future (BSF) initiative of Britain's New Labour government that began in 2003. This was an ambitious programme to address the deterioration in Britain's secondary school buildings and to ensure they were fit for the learning needs of students in the twenty-first century (Mahony and Hextall, 2013). The private finance arrangements were very complex, with capital funding coming to local authorities from the Department of Children, Families and Schools as PFI credits. Local authorities entered into Local Education Partnerships, which governed the development projects, with private sector partners and BSF Investments (a joint venture between the Department and Partnership UK, a public limited company part owned by HM Treasury and private sector investors that was responsible for furthering PPPs in the United Kingdom) (National Audit Office, 2009). The obscure and complex relationships between multiple partners were cited as the reason for the programme's disestablishment in 2011, but their relevance to this discussion is why the government adopted them in the first place, given that studies of PPPs suggest they deliver reduced outcomes on public benefit (Hodge and Greve, 2007).

The BSF initiative was associated with conceptualizing national education systems as the incubator of human capital so that 'enhanced skills and knowledge are deemed to play a key role in the global dynamics of economic competition between states' (Mahony et al., 2011, p. 346). In its early stages the benefit of the programme was touted by the government as a means to drive up educational standards through capital investment, with initial focus on the benefits of state-of-the-art equipment and facilities. However, the precise intended educational benefits were ambiguous, with many different and nuanced policy aims. Despite its contradictions:

> BSF constituted a genuine attempt to address the issues of poorly maintained and inadequate school premises across the board. At the same time it was also intended to make a difference to the quality of the community infrastructure within which schools are located. (Mahony and Hextall, 2013, p. 862)

Yet the programme was destined to be short lived with a change in government in 2010 where the priority shifted from educational benefit to efficiency and value for money, bringing it into closer alignment with expected benefits of PFIs.

In general the advantages of PFIs are the perceived benefits of competitive contracts, expected to drive down costs through competitive market tendering, transparency of process and transfer risk away from the public sector. In practice the compromises made in PPPs tend to mitigate competition, because the focus within them is on partnership and cooperation over a long period of time, oftentimes captured by elites or other groups and sometimes with raised costs (Landow and Ebdon, 2012). Risk is also less likely to be transferred away from the public sector within PFIs as private firms find ways to protect themselves from liability (ibid.), or government evaluation of the transfer of risk may be manipulated to justify a PPP rather than used in a transparent and neutral way (Khadaroo, 2014). The length of PPPs also works against the public interest, tying governments into contracts that restrict their capacity for future decision-making. The local education partnerships in the BSF programme were intended to govern the projects for over ten years (National Audit Office, 2009).

The rise of social enterprise and for-profit public benefit

As seen above in the discussions on corporate structure and charities, conditional public entities do not necessarily sit within the public sector. The legal forms for charities exist outside of the public sector for charitable purposes and must prove public benefit. Traditional corporate forms exist primarily to structure and regulate business practices, yet these forms may be adopted by an entity whose main purpose is for a public good. There are other forms, however, and a growing number of these are expressly designed for entities to work for the public good through the market. There is for business, according to a functionalist perspective, a role in social cohesion when social responsibility underpins its business practices, typically as social entrepreneurship (i.e. the activity of a change agent who attempts to create something of social value), or through social enterprise, business entities with social goals that primarily reinvest in their activities rather than maximize profit (Chell, 2007).

In the United Kingdom the discourse of enterprise was originally associated with a reduction in state welfare towards privatized public services, and the neoliberal enterprise culture of the Thatcher government that valued self-reliance and individual interest (Chell, 2007; Mason, Kirkbride and Bryde, 2007). As the culture of enterprise became embedded in practice and mind there was a natural migration towards social enterprise to pick up the services dropped by the public sector, opening them up to the risk of market competition, but tempered by a social ethics of business. The term social enterprise has come to represent an organization developed for the trading of services and products within the social economy, and where boundaries between for-profit and non-profit activities are blurred. 'Non-profit organisations are restricted from using trade as a means to raise capital, making them heavily dependent on donations and grants' (Mason et al., 2007, p. 286). A social enterprise is involved in trade and therefore can develop and grow as an organization through the exchange of products or services for capital. However, like a non-profit organization it has traditionally been constrained in how it distributes surplus, preventing distribution of profit to those who oversee the organization, including board members, directors or staff. Surplus instead must be returned to its core activity or stakeholders in the social issue it is designed to address. There are other differences between social enterprises and non-profit organizations. Governance type is another area where they may differ, so, for example, Low (2006) proposes that a stewardship model that empowers executives to make decisions to protect the interests of the owners or shareholders is more appropriate than a democratic model of governance often found in non-profit organizations. The assumption is executive decision-making is better for maximizing community interest when an organization is financially independent rather than grant dependent (Low, 2006). This insight is interesting to consider in respect of The Co-operative Bank's problems.

The rise of the social enterprise has also resulted in changes to legal structures. In the United Kingdom there is a new form of entity called the Community Interest Corporation (CIC). CICs are subject to Companies law and the CIC Regulations 2005 and were established to support social enterprise and other activities of benefit to the community. The CIC legislation offers an alternative to ordinary limited companies with no expectation of being motivated by profit or the need to seek charitable status (DfBEIS, 2016, p. 8). The CIC was the legal framework adopted in one of the authorities in my local authority study by a school-driven initiative to provide services to schools in the face of local authority cuts. Within this framework they were able to establish a co-operative social enterprise that was owned by member schools, any surplus profit returned to improve existing services or develop new services, or any further excess to be returned as a dividend to members to be redeployed in their work for the community.

However, an entity recently emerging in the United States challenges further the distinction between public and private interests. PBCs are types of entities that are both for-profit businesses designed to return investment to shareholders and fulfil a social function for public benefit. They emerged between 2010 and 2016 in thirty states and the District of Columbia (Glover et al., 2016), differentiated from a traditional company because maximizing wealth of shareholders is not their sole focus. 'The PBC laws are designed to empower the board of directors to consider additional stakeholders *alongside* shareholders, and leave it to the board to determine the relative weight to place on shareholders' and other stakeholders' interests' (ibid., p. 17). An example in education is Laureate Education, a for-profit provider of higher education that used the state of Delaware's PBC legislation to convert from a traditional corporation to a PBC. Laureate Education is based in the United States but has a global reach with higher education initiatives and partnerships in the Asia Pacific region, Europe, Latin America, Middle East, North America and Africa. Some of its partnerships are with notable public universities, such as University of Liverpool with whom it went into partnership to provide online programmes in 2007 while still operating with a traditional company structure (Spring, 2008). Discussing Laureate's decision to convert, its founder, chairman and CEO Douglas L. Becker made the following press statement:

> We recognized the enormous importance that society places on education as a public good. This inspired us to create a culture that combines the 'head' of a business enterprise with the 'heart' of a non-profit organization. (cited in Laureate Education, 2015)

This position is controversial on two fronts. Foremost, does a for-profit form permit public benefit at all? And second, even if it is accepted that the form can ideally serve a public benefit there may be uncertainty as to whether a PBC can be held to account for the realization of public benefit (Kurland, 2017). Tensions between profit-making and public benefit are examined in Chapter 5, picking this issue up again within the context of Laureate Education.

Mapping structural forms

This chapter set out to identify and map the forms adopted by educationally focused entities that aim to serve the public good from outside of the mainstream public sphere. Many of the entities that fall under this definition are commonly associated with privatization, and a retreat of the state sector from public education. The process of mapping must not undermine the exclusionary and fragmenting effects of the privatization of public education, but privatization is not just about the imposition of private interests. It represents a struggle between private and public interests that is important to examine in detail. Practices of publicness emerge to serve the interests of publics even within a privatized education system where public benefit is eroded or impoverished. While the state retreats from its public responsibilities, many people strive towards social justice and equality in different ways, adopting different structures and forms to govern and regulate their work. The purpose of mapping these entities is to open up conversation about public education in a way that might enable us to build democratically upon existing practices of publicness, rather than take recourse in a nostalgic view of a lost ideal public education. Identifying practices of publicness and their struggles with the limits placed upon them provides a basis from which to evaluate the quality of their publicness and the structures that support them. 'Strange, unfamiliar and complex issues are an enabling condition for democracy, and precisely because issues are difficult to resolve, we need to bring them out in public view' (Karlsson, 2006, p. 8). Putting up hard boundaries around privatized entities and dismissing their status as public institutions because of their involvement with private interests means that they become closed to public scrutiny. The privatization of entities puts at risk the diverse interests represented within them, some of whom are vulnerable to marginalization within mainstream public spheres. For example, the privatization of the domestic sphere has long marginalized women and positioned them as a concern outside of public interest.

A sympathetic reading of the entities examined in this chapter conceives of them as conditionally public, which highlights their public rather than private characteristics. This position is supportable by drawing upon a pluralist public sphere theory to recognize, on the one hand, limits to publicness of the state sector through neoliberal ideologies of state and processes such as economic globalization and technological advancement; and on the other the emergence of non-ideal publics that develop through publicness as relations between people and legitimate boundaries are established through circulating discourses and practices of self-organization (Warner, 2002; Abizadeh, 2012).

This chapter has discussed the structural forms used by self-organizing and emergent publics; it has grouped the different forms identified within four broad and overlapping categories. To summarize these categories include: (1) entities that work towards social goals for the good of members using well-established, corporate structures (predominantly co-operative and mutual structures); (2) entities that adopt structures specially designed for organizations concerned with public benefit and not business, including charities that are forms with a long history as well as new public benefit organizations; (3) PPPs where different partners have different goals and responsibilities in respect of profit-making, public benefit and risk; and (4) new kinds of entities such as social enterprise and for-profit PBCs that have been established with the intent to bring together public and private benefit. Further work would examine the quality of public education within these conditional public entities, assessing whether the compromises between public and private interests are worth making; however, some general conclusions that will be useful informing future work can be drawn from the process of mapping.

First, that there is a history of legal structures and governance forms that have been used to serve the public good beyond those we most commonly associate with public service, generally, and public education in particular, for example, public schools and state sector educational service units. The co-operative movement that developed alongside industrialization and beyond provides an alternative vision of economic exchange, and the importance of embedding humanistic values in co-operative entities. Yet even traditional corporate forms that exist to support the private financial interests of investors are used to serve the public good.

Second, as economic values have taken greater hold of social institutions and practices there has been expansion in the number and type of forms where both economic and social concerns meet. Public benefit organizations, CICs and PPPs represent the expanding field, and those establishing new entities or converting the old have complex choices to make about the type of structure that will support their mission.

Third, regardless of the social intent of an organization the intermeshing of public and private interests within conditional public entities forces them into relations of competition and opens them up to risks of economic failure. The example of the Co-operative Bank suggests that the capacity of conditional public entities to mitigate the risk may be hampered by their commitment to social goals. Organizations focused on public benefit may be rich in the resources of democratic governance, but these resources need to be offset by corporate governance skill sets when the organization has also adopted a corporate structure.

5

Public Benefit/Public Good

Organizations established for the public good may take many different forms, as we have seen in earlier chapters. While many organizations expressly concerned with the public good sit within what is commonly known as the public sector, there are entities that sit outside of this sector yet have a purpose that aims to further public interests. Even within common law the aim of public benefit is extended to organizations beyond the state sector. Typically, these are different kinds of entities that can be grouped together based on their adoption of a legal framework specially established for non-profit entities that pursue social goals (i.e. the broad category of charitable, not-for-profit and public benefit organizations that was discussed in Chapter 4). They are set up with the primary purpose of public benefit. While they are funded from outside of the state purse, any financial gain is redirected towards their primary purpose, and those involved in the organization as employees or trustees are limited in the extent to which they can personally profit from their involvement. These organizations have as their primary function and purpose the attainment of social goals, and thus educational institutions and organizations readily fit the bill. However, profit-making entities may also have as one of their purposes the pursuit of public benefit and therefore pursue educational goals alongside making money for investors. The U.S. for-profit Public Benefit Corporation legislation is one of the most recent legal frameworks established to form for-profit public benefit entities, but as will be seen in this chapter other kinds of entities that pursue public benefit also prioritize profit making, for example, profit-making private schools that choose to adopt a business framework such as a limited private company or partnership. Given the shifts in priorities towards commercial interests in education, entities that blur public and private goals are important to examine alongside those whose sole purpose is social or educational. How well do these different kinds of entities negotiate between private and public interests? To what extent does profit making get in the way of the public good?

The U.S. Public Benefit Corporation Laureate Education (2019) describes its mission to its investors as follows:

> Laureate Education is the world's largest global network of degree-granting higher education institutions. We believe in the power of education to transform lives and are committed to making a positive, enduring impact in the communities we serve. We believe that when our students succeed, countries prosper and societies benefit.

Laureate was identified by Altbach and Knight (2007) as part of the internationalization of higher education motivated by the large profits associated with knowledge industries. Ten years ago, they were reported to have 209,000 students (Naidoo, 2009). On their website in 2019 Laureate claims to have over 875,000 students in twenty-five institutions in fourteen countries. The largest number of institutions are in Brazil and Saudi Arabia. The institutions form the Laureate Education global network, and each offers a different set of educational programme. Yet all are held to account by the central corporation's code of conduct and ethics, based on the principle 'Here for Good'. Laureate states that in respect of the public good its 'specific benefit purpose is to produce a positive effect for society and students by offering diverse education programs both online and at campuses around the globe' (Laureate International Universities, n.d.). Yet the dominant good represented within the code of conduct does not seem to be a broad public good. Many of the statements are reiteration of personal or corporate legal responsibilities, and these and others are predominantly related to the good of the students as individuals, the good of the company and the good of its investors. This includes statements on issues such as fair and accurate record keeping, protecting the personal data of individuals, protecting Laureate's confidential information, not profiting from insider knowledge of Laureate and not taking or making bribes. In addition, the code of conduct stipulates that any media requests for information about Laureate must be directed to their public affairs or communication departments, indicating that individuals are not to speak publicly on behalf of the institution. This code of conduct and ethics is interesting to compare with the code of ethics from the University of Birmingham in England, which like most universities in British law is a corporation and exempt charity regulated by the independent public body the Office for Students, and therefore not-for-profit. Birmingham's code of ethics draws on the UK government's Nolan Committee's principles for holding office in public life: Selflessness, integrity, objectivity, accountability, openness, honesty and leadership. The foundation of these principles is to act in accordance with the public interest, and they have been adopted by many public entities in the United Kingdom. While there is in the United States an Office of Government Ethics, they have no statement on the ethical values for public life similar to the Nolan principles, and their codes of conduct reach only to the executive branch of its federal government. Like Laureate other universities within the jurisdiction of the United States develop and adopt their own ethical code of conduct and underpinning values. For example, the public university system (made up of a network of universities) University of California is committed to the ethical values of integrity in dealings with and on behalf of the university, excellence in work, accountability for ethical conduct and compliance with laws and University policy and respect for the rights and dignity of others. Stanford is a private university, but it operates on a not-for-profit basis and it too has a code of conduct underpinned by a set of ethical values:

> The University values integrity, diversity, respect, freedom of inquiry and expression, trust, honesty and fairness and strives to integrate these values into its education, research, health care and business practices. (Stanford, 2018)

Laureate, Stanford and the University of California are all similar and differ from the University of Birmingham in not making recourse to an abstract public good, where the public is conceived in the broadest terms as the general public. Yet both Stanford and the University of California engage with some idea of a differentiated public in their recognition of diversity and respect for others. The code of ethics from profit-making Laureate appears more centred on individualistic business rather than social ethics, for example, 'In the end, we are all responsible for our own behaviour.'

Like universities, most privately funded schools in England are charities rather than profit-making entities. Charity status confers the advantage of tax concessions (Fairburn, 2013). Unlike universities, private schools are not exempt charities and so they are regulated more rigorously than universities by the Charity Commission as well as the Department for Education Independent School Standards. Charity law means that the schools must therefore adhere to one or more of the purposes of charities (of which one is the advancement of education) and additionally contribute to public benefit. As discussed in previous chapters there has been considerable debate over the meaning of public benefit and how it can be achieved through the advancement of education within fee-paying schools (Millar, 2011; Fairburn, 2013). A case put before the Charities Tribunal by the Independent Schools Council (ISC), which is the largest body representing privately funded schools in the United Kingdom, led to clarification on the notion of public benefit (PASC, 2013) after the Charity Commission found two of five schools assessed for public benefit did not meet requirements. The revised definition of public benefit is that the charitable purpose must 'benefit the public in general, or a sufficient section of the public' and must 'not give rise to more than incidental personal benefit' (Charity Commission, 2013). There is also guidance from the Tribunal that the poor must not be excluded from benefit.

There is currently updated guidance from the Charity Commission on public benefit and recent guidance for trustees of state-funded schools. There is no guidance on public benefit specifically for privately funded schools beyond that which emerges through case law. In 2013, a report by the UK government's Public Administration Select Committee (PASC) suggested that the Charity Commission is asked to do too much and not sufficiently resourced to ensure public benefit from organizations awarded charitable status. Yet, comparing the notion of public benefit adopted by the Charity Commission with Labaree's definition of public good in education reveals it is an impoverished notion, and perhaps should not even be considered as more than individual benefit.

Study of privatization in state-funded schooling has increased awareness of how governance practices in individual schools contribute to and are enactments of the overall political organization of society. Privatization is generally perceived as a movement away from the public towards the private (Starr, 1988). Chapter 3 problematized the total exclusion of the public and its interests from our view of the private sector, recognizing both that by its nature the neoliberal state defines and restricts the public aspects of public institutions (Ball, 2009), and that expressions of democratic equality exist even within private sector schooling. We can investigate the problematic more extensively through a study of schools in England that are private in that they are generally funded by private sources and freed from many of the regulations of state-funded schooling, yet they still retain some commitment to the state through education, charity and company legislation. There are differences in private and state schools' relationship with the state, yet the privatization of state-funded schooling and policy debates in England that advocate for greater accountability of private schools may reduce the significance of these differences. Furthermore, some schools within the private sector deliberately construct for themselves an even closer relationship with the public good beyond the good of mainstream publics, encouraging discourse and deliberation on political, social and economic concerns among its citizenry, and may even act as Fraser's (1990) counterpublics where 'subordinated social groups invent and circulate counterdiscourses' (p. 67).

While the study drawn upon examined the public good within governance, curriculum pedagogy, intake and outcomes within the private schooling sector in England, this chapter is solely concerned with the extent and nature of governance for the public good. The governance of schooling is especially important because it offers opportunities for children and young people to practice democracy beyond what is possible from curriculum and pedagogical reform alone. Following Dewey (2016), education has an important role to play not just in preparing individuals to fulfil functions in society but also in preparing individuals to fulfil their roles in publics. When reconceptualizing public education an important element is provision of education in the processes through which deliberation and decision-making take place. This includes taking account of what is beyond the capability of an individual in a complex and pluralist society, so that education moves beyond the expectation that common schooling can inform public opinion in all things that matter, to lifelong and deeply embedded education that educates on the need to have an informed opinion and promotes engagement with specialized, systematized and expert knowledge.

Private schools and the public good are often seen as antithetical to one another; yet, investigations of private schooling can raise questions about the normative legitimacy of the state as a public sphere (Fraser, 2014) when the public sphere is conceived as multiple publics and private schools are conceived as potentially strong counterpublics that sit outside of weaker mainstream publics (Fraser 1990). The schools discussed below are rare within the generally elitist fee-paying private schooling sector in England, which caters to only 7 per cent of schoolchildren. The schools are different from other schools in private schooling because they aspire to mitigate or in some cases overcome the anti-democratic features of the sector. Elsewhere regarded as 'alternative' schools (Carnie, 2003; Kraftl, 2014), in this study such schools were considered of interest because they are on the one hand private, or set apart from society, yet on the other promote values for an equal and participatory society. They are also part of an established schooling sector, unlike their newly established counterparts in England, the state-funded independent, free and academy schools. The private schools discussed in this chapter are important locations in which we can investigate at close hand the limits to social justice when private interests are prioritized over the public good. These investigations contribute to our wider understanding of the nature of the public good in contemporary schooling.

Labaree's (1997) classification of the goals of schooling based on three competing views on the purpose of education helps to disentangle different notions of the public good within the studied schools. His democratic equality approach is related to Dewey's (1916) democratic ideal that promotes equality through equal exchange among diverse participants. The approach to schooling most favoured by policy makers, however, is a social mobility approach. Aspirations for social mobility are often driven by the desire for equality of opportunity, yet in practice policies of social mobility fuel competition and are fundamentally divisive. The chapter draws parallels between a social mobility approach and the way social equality is generally addressed within private schools. It explains how and to what extent private schools in England are governed by the state under the Independent School Standards (2010), corporate law and the majority held liable under the Charities Act, which requires them to demonstrate public benefit. The public good to which they are held accountable is limited, and very few of them demonstrate a commitment to a democratic public good. Yet the fact that some do hold themselves accountable to a democratic public is something that should not be ignored in critical analysis of public education.

Contested purposes of schooling

In his article on public versus private goods in American education, Labaree (1997) argues that politics is the underlying problem of education, because different ideological positions inform different practices and ultimately drive different goals for education. He identifies three alternative, ideologically driven approaches towards differing social outcomes for schooling: democratic equality, social efficiency and social mobility. His analysis helps to explain why different educational policies might adopt similar language that apparently supports social justice yet propose achieving social justice through such different means. It also provides tools with which to untangle the differences in intent and outcome of educational practices within single school sites.

The social efficiency approach to education focuses upon the development of a well-functioning and therefore highly specialized and differentiated society, typified by high-quality vocational education that aims to develop human productivity. He describes a social mobility approach as the perception that education 'is a commodity, the only purpose of which is to provide individual students with a competitive advantage in the struggle for desirable social positions' (p. 42). Labaree's argument is that the focus on 'individual status attainment' within a social mobility approach to schooling is even further removed from the public good than a conservative, social efficiency approach that values education for its contribution to the overall development of human capital. While the Nuffield Review of 14-19 Education and Training (2009) recommended diversifying curriculum and qualifications to more efficiently meet the specialist needs of complex, post-industrial Britain, the Conservative-Liberal Democrat Coalition government elected in 2010 focused upon elite curriculum and educational pathways for England.[1] While a new Conservative majority government has recently been elected in the United Kingdom, residual education policies of the last government for addressing disadvantage (like pupil premium funding that is targeted funding for supporting the attainment of individual children and the Progress 8 school performance measure that uses attainment data of select curriculum areas to provide a measure against which schools are compared) are a social mobility approach. Private schools that address social inequalities largely approach social advantage as an individual, private good that could be competed for with effort and ability (i.e. bursaries) or valued service learning primarily for the benefits it accrued the learner (Boyask, 2015c), and therefore are generally more closely aligned with Labaree's social mobility approach to schooling.

Labaree defines the goal of democratic equality to be the preparation of the young 'with equal care to take on the full responsibilities of citizenship in a competent manner' (p. 42). In a democratic equality approach to schooling it is regarded as in the public interest to educate the young in the deliberation, opinion formation and decision-making that they will require as full participants in democratic publics. In this approach governance plays an important role in education as a vehicle by which children and young people can practice democracy. The nature of democracy in education is fleshed out in Dewey's (1916) democratic ideal, which is taken to be the extent to which group members have 'an equable opportunity to receive and to take from others' and a 'large variety of shared undertakings and experiences' (p. 92), and there is 'not only freer interaction between social groups ... but change in social habit – its continuous readjustment through meeting the new situations produced by varied intercourse' (p. 94). His later work on the nature of the public concludes that the enhancement of democracy lies in strengthening its publics.

> The essential need, in other words, is the improvement of the methods and conditions of debate, discussion, and persuasion. That is the problem of the public. We have asserted that this improvement depends essentially upon freeing and perfecting the processes of inquiry and of dissemination of their conclusions. Inquiry, indeed, is a work which devolves upon experts. But their expertness is not shown in framing and executing policies, but in discovering

and making known the facts upon which the former depend. (Dewey, 2016, p. 225)

What we might expect to see therefore in schools that educate for public participation are schools that educate in public roles and responsibilities, and processes that encourage engagement with and direction of but not compliance with expert knowledge through the modelling and practice of governance.

Governance for the public good in private sector schooling

As previously discussed, within education we have seen in recent years an expansion of private involvement in state schooling, including the development of public–private partnerships (Robertson et al., 2012). This can be attributed to the desire to tap into what is perceived to be the innovation and efficiency of the private sector, while retaining some state regulation and central control for the purposes of equity (Lubienski, 2003; 2009). In England the growth of privatized schooling through the academies programme can be seen, which has resulted in a new type of semi-autonomous school that is publicly funded and privately governed through an academy trust (which is a charitable company made up of two tiers of governance: members of the trust and the board of governors). The separation within academies between funding from the state and management through the academy trust means they adhere to the OECD's (2012) definition of a private school that is 'managed directly or indirectly by a non-government organisation' (p. 18). Traditional private schools are further removed from some elements of state control, yet neither are they entirely deregulated. As discussed in Chapter 4 compared with non-state or private schools in other countries, the private schools of England and Wales receive comparatively a low level of state funding and are subject to a low level of regulation (Lubienski and Linick, 2011). There is heated debate on the limited contribution private schools make to the public good, and the Sutton Trust and Social Mobility Commission's (2019) report that identified that two fifths of the elite attended private schools highlight the entrenched social divisions between those who attend private and state-funded schooling. The government responds through changes in policy, most recently through Minister for Children and Families Nadhim Zahawi's July 2019 announcement that a scheme will be established for young people in care to identify opportunities to attend private schools. Yet the solutions proposed are inevitably limited because they are constructed from a social mobility perspective on schooling which accepts at its base inequality as an essential feature of society.

Private schools in England are subject to Schedule to the Education (Independent School Standards) Regulations 2014. These regulations outline the current expectations of private schools. The revisions made in 2014 and that came into force in 2015 included development of the standards for the spiritual, moral, social and cultural development of pupils. This included the development of a statement on the active promotion of British values, including: 'democracy, the rule of law, individual liberty, and mutual respect and tolerance of those with different faiths and beliefs'. While the previous version (2010) encouraged 'pupils to accept responsibility for their behaviour, show initiative and understand how they can contribute to community life', the 2014 Standards are more explicit in decreeing that individual pupils should themselves take responsibility for their school's public benefit by encouraging them to 'accept responsibility for their behaviour, show initiative and understand how they can contribute positively to the lives of those living and working in the locality in which the school is situated and to society more widely'. In consideration of this change it should be noted that the research reported below occurred before the change. It would be interesting to investigate whether private schools have adapted their responses to public benefit requirements since the change in standards. However, the motivator for the change in Standards was a crisis in diversity rather than a crisis in democracy. This is apparent from the Department of Education's (2019a) guidance on the inclusion of British values in the new Standards, which focuses on religious difference as a potential disruption to its democracy.

> A school is unlikely to meet the requirement in paragraph 2(b)(ii) if its policy on curriculum or the supporting plans and schemes of works, for example:
>
> a. include material in history lessons which promotes non-democratic political systems rather than those based on democracy, whether for reasons of faith or otherwise;
> b. teach that the requirements of religious law permit the requirements of English civil or criminal law to be disregarded;
> c. are designed to suggest to pupils that some or all religions are wrong and that therefore those who follow them are not worthy of respect. For the avoidance of doubt, teaching that some religions, all religions, or atheism/agnosticism are wrong does not conflict with fundamental British values, so long as it is made clear that adherents of those belief systems should be treated with respect. (DfE, 2019a)

The strengthening of democracy through enhanced contribution to the public good appears secondary; however, the guidance also includes advice on promoting respect for others and understanding and recognition of difference, with especial regard for the Equality Act 2010.

While one of the main arguments of advocates for private sector involvement in schooling is that it promotes innovation, empirical evidence from privatized state-funded schools shows that they are less likely than public counterparts to innovate (Lubienski, 2009). Following the argument that private sector involvement enhances innovation, private schools have not shown themselves to be especially innovative either, particularly in respect of promoting democracy. The structure of the school is one way that a school might express its difference from others. As discussed in an earlier chapter the Standards allow for schools to be managed and led by a proprietor who has overall responsibility for the school to meet its statutory requirements, and the proprietor might be an individual or a body of individuals incorporated or unincorporated. In practice the structures of private schools are more similar even than the legislation allows.

A significant majority of private schools are charities rather than for-profit entities. Charity status gives some tax advantages to schools (Fairburn, 2013). This includes tax breaks for the schools themselves, such as business rates relief, and also tax relief for those paying school fees because they are exempt from VAT. To accrue the advantage of charitable status, a private school must demonstrate charitable purpose. While the advancement of education is a recognized charitable purpose, the education of a private elite is not enough because it does not fulfil charity law requirement of public benefit. For a school to claim its charitable purpose is the advancement of education it must also 'benefit the public in general, or a sufficient section of the public' and must 'not give rise to more than incidental personal benefit' (Charity Commission, 2013).

There is recent guidance for trustees of state-funded schools on public benefit, but there continues to be no guidance on public benefit specifically for private schools beyond that which emerges through case law. When the Charity Commission found in 2010 two of five private schools assessed for public benefit did not meet requirements, the ISC put a case before the courts that included complaints from the schools that the requirements for public benefit were unstated and therefore unfair. The Charities Tribunal considered what constituted a sufficient section of the public, and whether beneficiaries could be those who can afford to send their children to private schools (Fairburn, 2013). The Tribunal refused to give any definitive answer, suggesting that individual circumstances would dictate what was and what was not sufficiently to the public benefit. The Tribunal did conclude that a school's charitable status was dependent upon what it was set up to achieve not on what it presently does, and that trustees should decide on what is appropriate public benefit within their particular circumstances. They issued guidance that the poor must not be excluded from benefit and claimed that a charitable private school would not be acting for public benefit if it only acted in the interests of its fee-paying students. In the absence of any clear guidance other than the stipulations about ensuring the poor are not excluded from benefit and that schools should provide benefit to more than fee-paying students, public benefit has largely been interpreted by school trustees as the offer of bursaries towards the fees of those who could not otherwise afford to attend, or support for the social mobility of a minority. The report by the PASC claimed that the legal battles had weakened the Charity Commission, and defining public benefit was beyond its present resources and put its role as regulator in jeopardy. The Charity Commission is limited in its capacity to provide oversight of private schools' commitment to public benefit, both in law and in practice. The hands-off approach of the Charity Commission in both its refusal to define public benefit and limited oversight of public accountability due to restrictions in its resourcing might make it appear ideologically neutral, yet similarities in the way public benefit is interpreted suggest there are strong normalizing influences upon private schools. A future study may investigate public benefit and how it is shaped by charity law. The research reported here, however, shows that in some rare cases public benefit is interpreted by private schools as benefit for a democratic public. It is also possible for an ideology of democratic equality to inform how a private school interprets its public accountability through corporate law.

In recent years the move towards blurring of public and private entities through privatization, quasi-markets and social enterprise has resulted in the development of new forms of legal structure that are specifically intended to further social aims. As discussed in Chapter 4 Community Interest Corporations (CIC) are a new company type that appeared in 2005, and in 2013 Charitable Incorporated Organizations (CIO) emerged, a new regulatory structure for schools who wish to operate as charities, providing an alternative to registering as both company and charity. There is also a rapidly growing interest in the school sector in mutuals and co-operative trusts as a means to administer charities and limited companies. The schools in this study tend to predate these changes and therefore have more traditional structures, yet there is some indication that the chosen structure is correlated to participation in school governance at the schools, which has been interpreted in this study as evidence of democratic 'equal and free exchange' between different members of the school community in school decision-making (Dewey, 1916). The research reported in this chapter sought private schools that demonstrated some form of commitment to democratic equality within the five dimensions of governance, curriculum, pedagogy, school intake and outcomes (at societal, school and student levels). While each of the dimensions investigated should contribute to achieving the political aspirations of democratic equality, governance is particularly important to this goal because it educates through providing children and young people with the opportunity to practice within an authentic context of democratic citizenship as well as modelling the procedures of democratic governance.

Conditional equality in private schooling: A research study

The research which this chapter draws upon was a desk-based study that developed understanding iteratively and in response to the problematic of conflicts between public and private interests in state-funded independent schools and traditional private schooling, following a pragmatic line of inquiry (Biesta and Burbules, 2003). The inquiry started with a review of the available websites of all private schools in England (n=1,924) to identify only those schools that publicly express a commitment to principles of equality and participation as they are characterized in Dewey's (1916) democratic ideal. The schools were categorized on the basis of this review as excluded, included or requiring further investigation. For a school to be included evidence was sought in these data of statements that resonated with Dewey's (1916) democratic ideal as it has been defined earlier in this book. To state simply, evidence was sought that the school had a commitment to equal and free exchange within some kinds of relationships between different members within the schools (internal relationships) and/or in equal and free exchange in the relations between the school and external groups, particularly others who differ from those within their school community (external relationships). It is recognized that an expression of equality is not the same as the enactment of equality, and that the data are limited to providing only an indication of the extent of democratic ideals in private schooling. This was a small-scale study with limited resources, but what the chosen method lacked in depth it made up for in reach.

The data collection began with a single search in EduBase (Department for Education database of schools) selecting 'Independent schools' as type of school, and 'open' and 'open, but proposed to close'. Only schools in England and not the other three nations of the United Kingdom were selected. This search identified 1,924 private schools collected on one day (in case of changes over time) that were entered into a database along with the identifying details held in EduBase. As the research continued, it became apparent that some schools in this database were misclassified; that is, some were included when they were not independent schools, and more problematically, some independent schools were classified wrongly so they did not show up in the initial search. One school subsequently found and included in later stages of the research is identified. Once the records were entered into the database, each school name was put into Google so that the website of the school could be reviewed. Some websites were very straightforward to find (and the schools were verified via the postcodes to make sure it was the right school). Others required the postcode to be put into the search engine in order to find the website. There were 182 schools with no websites and these were excluded from the study. This was a particular issue for faith schools; only one Jewish school had a website, and many Islamic schools didn't have websites. Another thirty-one schools were excluded because appropriate information was not accessible from their website (e.g. website down, website in a foreign language, website had little information). This left 1,711 schools in the survey.

The starting point was looking for a statement on the ethos of the school. In most cases the website had a page which was titled 'ethos', 'philosophy', 'aim', 'vision' or 'values'. If this was not obvious, the internal search engine for the site was used and searched for these terms. Sometimes this turned up results in the school's prospectus or website. The history, intake policy, funding and any other pertinent information was also reviewed. These were compared with Dewey's (1916) democratic ideal. To help recognize democracy in actual rather than ideal publics (Fraser, 1990), websites were also compared with a statement of philosophy taken from a 'standard' school, that is, standard in the sense it provided a normative reference point against which other schools could be compared, rather than an ideal type of democratic school. This school was the democratic school, Sands, investigated in a previous case study of democratic publics in private schooling (Boyask, 2013). This previous study helped inform the criteria for inclusion of schools used in the larger study. Sands School was not an archetype, because like other schools in the private sector there were limits to its democracy, yet because its inclusion was established it provided an important benchmark against which to examine whether other schools were more or less democratic in their ethos.

It became apparent through the survey that the final category was necessary for schools that express or realize their commitment to equality in ways unanticipated by the researchers, thereby raising the need for inductive analysis as well as a straightforward comparison. This was the case for some schools with a faith ethos where equal relations were conditional upon supplication to a higher authority, which were each assessed on a case-by-case basis, and also for the many private schools that offered service learning, described by Dymond et al. (2013) as a way for students to learn through 'authentic, hands-on projects that connect their learning to the real world' (p. 293). It was concluded that in most of the cases examined, relationships in service learning were not equable and therefore generally not used as grounds for inclusion in this study. This was generally because the private school students, who were in a privileged position themselves, gave service to others who were perceived to be less fortunate. Schools that obviously showed no especial commitment to equality were marked as not being included in the study. Those which seemed as if they might be candidates for further study were assigned a 'maybe' status and their websites were examined in greater depth and discussed to arrive at the decision whether to include in the study.

The schools that were categorized as included were then put into a new spreadsheet. The websites were revisited to clarify the basis for selection. The reasons for inclusion were then grouped into five themes: governance, pedagogy, curriculum, intake and outcomes. Each school could have information in any of these themes, and there also could be conflicting reasons for inclusion or exclusion across the themes (i.e. one school could have a 'yes' in governance, but a 'no' in intake). Through this process sixty-four schools were identified for which there was a case for inclusion from our data source (which was limited to what a school publicly expresses about its practice on its own website) within at least one of the five themes. In other words, 3.7 per cent of private schools publicly expressed on a school website commitment to equality within our terms of reference.

The next phase of the research was to select schools for case study from the sixty-four included schools. The case studies were also desk-based and data collection consisted of developing case files from publicly accessible documentary sources (such as websites, school census data, inspection reports, school prospectuses, newspapers, instruments of government, public benefit and annual financial reports, and extant research) and telephone interviews with school leaders, governors or administrators. The case studies did not involve direct observation of practices at the schools, which could be seen as a limitation of the data collected, though direct observation within case study may also distort findings through problems of perception and researcher bias (Hammersley et al., 2002).

The case studies were developed on a premise that general understanding can be developed through theoretical inference (Gomm et al., 2002). The intention was to gather enough data or raw materials from which to construct new knowledge about how the school intended to work towards equality within one of the five dimensions of governance, pedagogy, curriculum, intake and outcomes, and through correspondence with the context of private schooling and how that has been understood theoretically (Biesta and Burbules, 2003). This meant that the case studies were not constructed according to external rules about what data must be collected, but were developed on the basis of what was available that was of use to the particular issues of interest within that case study school.

The decision to include a school for case study was made through discussion within the research team, identifying significant features of the schools and the different ways that they met the conditions for inclusion in the study. The schools were grouped, resulting in seventeen different types of school that varied in how they realized their commitment to democracy through the school's responsibility to wider society, the way the school was organized, leadership of the school, the schools' approaches to inclusion, how the school managed its financial commitments and school definitions of learning. Schools were selected for case study from each of the seventeen groupings. The number of case studies increased to eighteen when it was realized that one of the schools that had been expected to turn up in the list of included schools had not been identified in the initial review and represented an approach to equality that had not been recognized in any other schools. Following up on this point it seemed that the school had been classified in EduBase as an 'Other Independent Special School' (which were not included in the original review) despite it not conforming to the EduBase glossary definition, which is a school that caters 'wholly or mainly for children with statutory statements of special educational needs'.

The identification of such a limited number of schools in the initial review raised important ethical questions regarding confidentiality and anonymity. In most cases the schools have very specific characters, and it would be impossible to say much that was meaningful about such well-known schools if it was a condition to maintain anonymity. The available data were also specific to the school because of the special character of these schools, and not in the regular formats of data returned for state-funded schools. For example, not all private schools participate in national qualifications, meaning that achievement data may or may not map onto national attainment data. With little available statistical information about the schools, some data had to be requested directly from schools, through interviews responding to what was available in each case and adapting information sheets to suit. Of the eighteen case study schools, eight agreed to participate in an interview. Individuals are not identified within the study, and any personally identifiable information (including restricted data) is aggregated or obscured. Schools are identifiable.

Governance in the case study schools

The list of the eighteen case study schools, including the dimensions in which the case study schools were included and identified as having a commitment to equality and participation, and summary of type of data collected are listed in Table 5.1.

All the documentary evidence was sourced, analysed and the salient information entered into spreadsheets, while the original documents are held on file. The spreadsheets hold demographic information about the schools, references to existing study and literature (in particular Carnie (2003) which mentions a number of the case study schools) and quotations from the documents and interviews selected because they illuminate how the schools enact their philosophies within the five dimensions of governance, curriculum, pedagogy, intake and outcomes. The development of these case files formed the first phase of analysis.

The next phase of analysis looked across the schools at the five dimensions. The analysis of the case studies presented here is within the area of school governance, because as described above governance is most closely associated with the goals of democratic equality and presents opportunities for students' authentic engagement in democratic publics. Each of the other four dimensions has also been analysed and reported upon (Boyask, 2015b). The findings on school governance have been extended into an ongoing investigation of the nature of the public in present-day English schooling that includes and goes beyond the private schools discussed in this chapter, using an extended case methodology that looked for patterns and points of significance emerging from the data and exploring these insights through appropriate theoretical frames (Burowoy, 1998).

Figures from the ISC indicate that of their member schools 82 per cent are charities and 16 per cent are profit-making (ISC, 2013). Of the case study schools, sixteen, or 89 per cent had opted for charity status, and therefore were required by the Charities Act to demonstrate public benefit. Two of the schools (The Acorn School and Summerhill School) chose not to adopt charity status and therefore

Table 5.1 The eighteen case study schools

Name of School	Foci of the Case Study bold indicates main focus *italics* indicates limited data	Data Collected	
		Documents	Interviews
The Acorn School	*Governance*, **Curriculum**, **Pedagogy**, *Intake*, **Outcomes**	✓	
Ackworth School	Curriculum, *Pedagogy*. **Intake**, **Outcomes**	✓	
Dame Catherine Harpur's School	**Governance**, Intake, Outcomes	✓	
The Dharma School	Governance, Curriculum, **Intake, Outcomes**	✓	
Educare Small School	Curriculum, Outcomes	✓	✓
Latymer Upper School	Curriculum, **Outcomes**	✓	✓
Lewes New School	**Governance**, *Curriculum*, Pedagogy, Outcomes	✓	✓
The Mohiuddin Girls School and College	*Curriculum, Intake*	✓	
New Forest Small School	Curriculum, Pedagogy	✓	✓
Peaslake School	**Governance**, Intake	✓	
St Christopher's School (Letchworth)	**Governance**, Intake, **Outcomes**	✓	✓
Sands School	**Governance**, Curriculum, Outcomes	✓	
The Small School	Governance, **Curriculum, Pedagogy,** Outcomes	✓	✓
The Stephen Perse Foundation	**Governance**, *Pedagogy*, Intake, Outcomes,	✓	
Summerhill School	*Governance*, Curriculum, Pedagogy, Intake, **Outcomes**	✓	✓
The Treehouse School	**Governance**, Intake	✓	✓
York Steiner	**Governance**	✓	
Young Gloucestershire Youth Achievement Foundation	Governance, *Curriculum*, Intake, Outcomes	✓	

have no requirement to show public benefit. These two schools are least tied to the state of all the case studies yet represent quite different manifestations of governance. Summerhill is notable for the participation of students in governing the school, offering us a vision of Fraser's (1990) strong counterpublics constructed outside of the weaker mainstream public sphere of the state. 'We are a self-governing community, which means that the whole group makes all the decisions regarding our daily lives in the school' (Summerhill FAQs, 2009, p. 8). There are, however, limits to the participation of the students. 'The business side, the hiring and firing of staff, intake of pupils etc. are not the responsibility of the community although input is always available and welcome' (Summerhill FAQs, 2009, p. 8). At the Acorn School there was no evidence found of commitment to participation in its governance beyond the company proprietors, even though it is evident in other aspects of its operation. The Acorn School's annual return to Companies House in 2012 reveals that the school is a private company limited by shares, which is potentially a profit-making structure and is directed solely by the Head Teacher and school bursar.

The majority of the remaining case study schools had opted for a Private Company Limited by Guarantee structure, that until recently had been the company structure most commonly adopted for non-profit organizations. An exception was St Christopher School (Letchworth) that has a share model of business (Private Company Limited by Shares) that is potentially profit-making and is the same company structure as The Acorn School. At St Christopher School (Letchworth) and unlike The Acorn School, its charity status excludes profit-making.

The sixteen schools that are charities have a range of approaches to governance. This includes Sands and York Steiner that appear to extend their commitment to participation and democracy to their governance structures, widening the range of participants included in the opinion formation and decision-making that constitutes Fraser's (1990) strong democratic publics. These aspirations are expressed in publicity material and on their websites, but the schools are particularly noteworthy because they embed their commitments to equality in governance within their legal documentation (such as instrument of government, and financial and public benefit reports). Other schools used standard legal templates or perfunctory language. Yet there is a significant difference between Sands and York Steiner schools, because at Sands they deliberately engage students in governance:

> In accordance with the Conduct of the School as laid out in its Instrument of Government, School management is effected by discussion and consensus

and due regard is taken by the Governors of the views and wishes of the staff and pupils on all matters relating to the management, conduct and underlying philosophy of the School and behaviour in the School. (Sands School Trustees' Report and Financial Statements for the Year Ended, 31 July 2012)

Whereas at York Steiner statements made about governance are limited to the participation of adults within the school community.

> The revised management structure continues to bring improvements in accountability, flow of communication and governance. Parental skills are being widely used in management bodies, resulting in improved management and decision-making. The College of Teachers continues to ensure the spiritual essence of Steiner education remains strong and that pedagogical support, advice and guidance is available to all within the school. (York Steiner Annual Report and Financial Statements for the year ended, 31 August 2012)

At Sands their democratic philosophy leads them to include students in most but not all forms of decision-making at the school, aligning with the educational goals of Labaree's (1997) democratic equality, whereas at York Steiner governance is distributed only among teachers, parents and other adults within the school community and incorporated into operational management. Democracy in the governance at St Christopher School (Letchworth) appears more limited, although is targeted towards students. The school promotes a form of self-government that includes a School Council of senior pupils, whole school meetings and pupil observers who observe class teaching and provide teachers with feedback (according to written notes on self-government from 2012 provided by the school). The following are examples of decisions that have been made through self-government:

> Among the issues that have been settled by Council in the last decade have been the structure of the Council and its constitution, the establishment of the 'Coffee Shop', the setting up of a system to give grants to clubs and societies, the refinement of the caution money system to compensate both individuals and the School for unattributed damage, the abolition of the caution money system, the establishment of an annual summer fair, the making compulsory of the School meeting, the banning of South African produce in the 1980s but not those of Nestle in the 1990s after hearing both sides of the argument, the use of the school minibuses and the carrying of a banner at an anti-war demonstration. (Notes on Self-Government from school, 2012)

While the Council can make recommendations to school leaders and governors, the self-government system is largely removed from the main governance, leadership and management structures at the school. The Head can veto any policies emanating from the School Council.

Evidence of participation in governance was sought not just in respect of members of the school community but also the extent to which the school encouraged free exchange with others from social groups different from itself. Dewey (1916) claims that interchange between different social groups is a feature of a democratic society.

> The more activity is restricted to a few definite lines – as it is when there are rigid class lines preventing adequate interplay of experiences – the more action tends to become routine on the part of the class at a disadvantage, and capricious, aimless, and explosive on the part of the class having the materially fortunate position. (p. 81)

Governance and oversight through a representative and democratically elected local government should theoretically ensure schools also engage with difference externally through administration and governance practices. While St Christopher's School (Letchworth) clearly intended to have a disinterested group of governors who 'represent a range of skills and experiences, developed in different walks of life, enabling them to contribute ideas, to make judgments and to see the School's work in a wider context' (School website, accessed 10 June 2013) the majority of the governors in 2012/13 had a close connection with the school, either as present or past parents or former pupils.

The governance structure at Lewes New School requires that 50 per cent of the governing body is made up of parents and current or former teaching staff. Lewes New School also enshrines a special responsibility for trustees from outside the direct school community, yet it has also drawn them from niche, arguably elite, groups such as the spiritual group Subud, Guerrand-Hermès Foundation for Peace and the professoriate. It is difficult to argue that they interrupt the 'rigid class lines' as required within a Deweyan democracy. This commonality of social class is even more pronounced within the Stephen Perse Foundation in respect of governance. It has an outreach programme working with state-funded partner schools on projects of curriculum and pedagogy. There is also evidence of some engagement with outside organizations in its external governance relationships; however, the school's relationship is with colleges of the University of Cambridge and thus it may be argued these are relations between elite equals rather than an extension of democracy to groups unlike itself.

The extent and nature of the public good

Private schooling is an established education market in which we can examine at close hand what happens when aspirations for democratic equality are played out within an education context dominated by relations of consumption and performativity. Following Fraser's (1990) redefinition of the 'public' as multiple publics of differing strengths, we should also recognize the public dimensions of private organizations lest they are entirely set apart from public scrutiny and critical analysis. It is also the case that private organizations are not necessarily weaker publics than the public as it has been institutionalized within the state and what we know as public education. Wahlström (2010) implies that Fraser's publics extend to all who are affected by a governance structure. In the case of transnational developments in education policy, these structures may be supranational, but in other cases such as the governance structures of individual schools they may be quite localized publics. The strength of such publics is dependent on 'the force of public opinion' and whether 'a body representing it is empowered to translate such 'opinion' into authoritative decisions' (Fraser, 1990, p. 75). Furthermore, recognition and resultant analysis of the publicness of private institutions may provide opportunities for their redefinition along democratic lines.

The survey of private schools in England (n=1,711) revealed that sixty-four schools (3.7%) publicly express a commitment to principles of equality and participation as defined by the terms of reference outlined above. The main criterion for inclusion in the study was Dewey's democratic ideal. It was evident through the review of websites, however, that private schools address social inequality through a number of means, and not all were recognized as grounds for inclusion. Excluded schools typically engaged students in service learning, where the service providers were the main beneficiaries, and offered bursaries based on merit. What distinguished the included schools from these schools were differences in their conceptualization of educational goals. The sixty-four schools included in this study, because they express some commitment to democratic equality, are working both within and against the limits of educational policy, and furthermore within and against the limits of the educational market. Their position is evidently precarious, and it is noteworthy that since this research began three of the eighteen case study schools have closed (although one of these has found a new place for itself as a state-funded free school).

That 96.3 per cent of privately funded schools did not obviously display a commitment to a democratic public good may not be unsurprising to either proponents or opponents of private schooling, but it is an important figure to contemplate. There is clearly little diversity in respect of the political drivers within the private schooling sector, even though the private sector generally is represented as a site of innovation and novelty compared with the sluggish and conservative state (Mazzucato, 2013). The main ties to the state for private schools are through the Independent School Standards (2010) and, for those who adopt charity status, charity law. Charity law in England is particularly interesting because it includes the explicit requirement for schools to demonstrate public benefit, albeit largely leaving the schools themselves to define the nature of public benefit. The survey of schools found a similarity of approach to public benefit among most private schools, including the promotion of service learning, fee relief through bursaries and, in some cases, wider community use of the school facilities. The similarity of approach was even evident among those schools included in the study, and of those with charity status only a few went beyond this approach to demonstrate clear evidence of democratic governance. The lack of diversity suggests that some process outside of the legislative framework, which is so loosely defined, is driving approaches to public benefit. The commonality of approach warrants additional investigation to understand its origins. Initial thoughts are that there are hidden coercive practices of governance acting upon the schools through an enmeshing of the regulatory discourses of state and market.

The public is not restricted to schools that have opted for charity status. The two case study schools that opted out of charity status have quite different governance structures and approaches to student engagement even though they are both profit-making businesses. The Acorn School makes a clear distinction between governance by the proprietors and equality for pupils enacted through curriculum and pedagogy. Summerhill also distinguished between the business practices of the school and the role of students, but did engage students in forms of self-government that would prepare them for the citizenship roles envisaged by Labaree (1997) in his democratic equality approach to schooling. The included schools that show evidence of democracy, and support opinion formation and decision-making in their governance practices go beyond Charity Commission requirements to demonstrate public benefit, whether they have charitable status or not.

The effects of charity law are closer to Labaree's (1997) individualistic and competitive social mobility approach than democratic equality. This is a restricted notion of the public good that focuses upon the advancement of individuals who have experienced financial disadvantage and shows how the legislative state is enmeshed with the market. By restricting its influence on the most vulnerable in society it conforms to a market view of the state as a safety net against market failure (Robertson et al., 2012; Mazzucato, 2013).

So, if the neoliberal state is not intending to support democratic equality, then how should we conceptualize private schools with loosened ties to the state that are intending to support democratic equality? Fraser (1990) offers us a rationale for conceptualizing schools outside of the mainstream as potentially strong counterpublics, a view that is supported by a relative understanding of notions of public and private (Wilson, 2012), differentiating between the state and the public and engaging with the complexities of the actual rather than idealized public sphere. Fraser's conceptualization of counterpublics within actually existing democracies, and her provocative suggestion that self-managed institutions outside of direct state control may provide sites in which to develop strong, alternative publics is a potential way of describing these schools.

While Fraser's (1990) depiction of multiple and polyvocal publics that exist both within and outside of the state offers a novel way of conceptualizing private schools, care must be taken with this concept. Institutions outside of the state, an institutionalized public sphere, are not necessarily the strong counterpublics envisaged by Fraser. While the schools included in this study show some alignment with a democratic ideal, none of the schools in this study conformed to that ideal. They vary in the extent to which they address equality through their governance practices, and some showed no particular commitment to democratic governance or may promote elitism through governance structures. The contradictory drivers within these private school sites mean that they, like the mainstream public sphere where its policies of modernization have been built from the limited public participation of an impoverished democracy, are limited forms of public. The advantage, however, of conceptualizing schools like the included private schools as counterpublics is that it provides a means to retain sight of the educational goal of democratic equality, even when this goal is disregarded as a legitimate goal for schooling within the neoliberal state.

Note

1 Education policy is devolved to governments within each of the four nation states of the United Kingdom. The Westminster government of the United Kingdom has responsibility only for educational policies in England.

6

Pluralist Public Accountability

Public accountability in educational policy tends to employ a very limited view of the public, that is, it implies being held accountable to a unified and essential public whose interests are realized through the state. The notion of pluralist, unbounded mainstream and counterpublics is an important addition to discussion of public accountability in education. Conceptualizing publics as unbounded or pluralist extends public interest to wider, complex and more inclusive formations of publics and their constituents. Public accountability in a pluralist context should extend beyond accountability to the public defined through national boundaries, because national boundaries create unjust exclusions. Yet without clear boundaries to a public it is more difficult to conceptualize where accountabilities lie. Conceptualization of publics as emergent and multiple can be associated with relations between individuals and social groups that are mutually constitutive rather than oppositional (Yeatman, 2007; 2015). In a social model of individualistic collectivism, public accountability changes from a relationship of authoritarian control to one of reciprocity where individuals work co-operatively towards collective good. Yet there are many and varied challenges to realizing the public good through mutual relations. This chapter discusses the challenges of constituting publics through individualistic collectivism initially theoretically but then as the challenges are experienced within the realpolitik of schooling. It then explores the implications of these challenges for public accountability. It draws upon research within a private democratic school that exhibits properties of a conditional counterpublic sphere. The research provides an illustration of co-operative individualism within a self-governing school that negotiates a compromise between values of democracy and autonomy as it is held to account concurrently by larger and more authoritarian governance formations.

Unlike the argument presented in Chapter 2 to define the limits of a public through subjection to the practices of self-governance, the limits of the public in public systems of schooling tend to be predefined through regional or national boundaries. This is the case even though such boundaries produce exclusions and inequalities especially for mobile populations or stateless peoples. Some recent dilemmas in Europe such as the migrant crisis and Brexit illustrate the limits of defining the right to schooling through national citizenship. A recent UNICEF report (Refugee Support Network, 2018) on equality and access to education of refugee and asylum-seeking children in England and Wales shone a light on a series of inequalities to which they were subject, including lengthy waiting lists for schooling and services, declining numbers of expert personnel working in local authorities and reluctance of schools to admit upper-secondary school students due to the fear they will negatively affect overall school examination profiles. We can see here boundaries predefining the legitimacy of an apparently democratic public and its right to participate in governance, but therefore not accommodating all those subjected to its self-rule. Public education is associated with citizenship, but not necessarily democratic citizenship.

Free and universal education has become more pervasive globally, and state-funded school systems of parliamentary or other forms of democracy are remarkably similar structurally to those of authoritarian nations. Education that prepares children for their role in state is also a necessary tool of neoliberalism. One of the paradoxes of neoliberalism is that while it is a philosophy of individual freedom achieved through the loosening of external and authoritarian control, it too is dependent upon the authority of government. Nation states influenced by neoliberalism tend to condense governmental power in an executive, and correspondingly weaken government in other branches (Yeatman, 2015). For example, a neoliberal dynamic can be seen in the removal of resources from local government in England. Strong control by central government and weakening of local government is a recurrent theme in neoliberal policy and can be observed in the many and varied forms of privatization. Accompanying the expansion of privatization in education, whether that is self-governing schools or fully private educational entities, there is a visible shift in the locus of power towards the centre. We can see this in education policy tools of central government such as inspectorates, qualification frameworks, national curricula and publication of school attainment scores which hold to account individual educators, educational leaders and their institutions (Keddie, 2018; Verger et al., 2019).

Domination by a neoliberal government and its repression of state citizens because of its relationship to market relations is of a different order from that embedded within traditional conceptualizations of state authority, which is overtly centralist. Neoliberal government is dependent upon the flattening of distinctions between market and state. Yeatman (2015) suggests that the governmentality of a neoliberal state is based in a responsibility for maintaining and overseeing the rules of conduct and the mechanisms for enforcing them that are inherent in a market mode of social engagement. Rather than assuming overt power neoliberal governments make it appear that power is centred in the individual, and the domination of government hidden (Yeatman, 2015). The responsibility for living by those rules is pushed out to individuals who are subject to responsibilization (Rawolle et al., 2017; Keddie, 2018). Responsibilization is associated with the individualization of late modern societies, which is based upon the management of risk. However, concepts of individualization and responsibilization differ, and some are more pessimistic about making individuals responsible for decisions on the many different facets of their lives and their capacity to carry them out (Rawolle et al., 2017). Writing in the context of the ecological challenges facing society Beck (1996) argued that nature has become inseparable from society and ecological crisis is integrally bound up with conflicts over nationality, ethnicity and resources. Risks within a context of late capitalism and ecological crisis are according to Beck 'hard to manage dangers' rather than quantifiable risks. There is no exact science of determining risk or predicting outcomes. In a neoliberal individualized society it is individuals who must negotiate the crises of nature – state – market and make decisions for themselves.

> The ethic of individual self-fulfilment and achievement is the most powerful current in modern society. The choosing, deciding, shaping human being who aspires to be the author of his or her own life, the creator of an individual identity, is the central character of our time. (Beck and Beck-Gernsheim, 2002, pp. 22–3)

Yet for Beck rather than empowerment the choices of individuals are in the main forced choices that arise through the dissolution of social structure and cohesion (Beck, 1996; Beck and Beck-Gernsheim, 2002; Rawolle et al., 2017).

> The social structure of the global life of one's own thus appears together with continual differentiation and individualization – or, to be more precise, with the individualization of classes, ethnic groups, nuclear families and normal female biographies. In this way, the nationally fixed social categories of industrial society are culturally dissolved or transformed. They become 'zombie categories', which have died yet live on. Even traditional conditions of life become dependent on decisions; they have to be chosen, defended and justified against other options and lived out as a personal risk. Not only genetically modified food but also love and marriage, including the traditional housewife marriage, become a risk. (Beck and Beck-Gernsheim, 2002, p. 27)

A more optimistic view of individuals can be found in the writing of Yeatman (2007). She highlights a political struggle at work in late modernity between different forms of individualism. A conflict arises as delegitimized, self-sufficient patrimonial individualism has been challenged by subjective, interdependent, postpatrimonial individualism. The subjective individual is based in a 'conception of the individual as an embodied subject or self' (Yeatman, 2007, p. 55) who is interconnected with others, lives life creatively and is associated with participatory democracy within a highly differentiated society. Beck sees as the conclusion of a differentiated society enforced individualization and inequality as the majority fail to attain subjecthood through the successful negotiation of manufactured risk. Yeatman conceives of an inclusive alternative where individualization leads to an interdependent individual in a differentiated society, although she also recognizes inequalities in the attainment of subjecthood. Authority for self-rule is achieved through jurisdictional sovereignty. Herein lies the struggle between individualisms. A gap between the emergence of a collective and unregulated self and its limited realization of which institutional forms could support its sovereignty has created the space for a patrimonial self to adapt to its challenge. In the 'transitional void' a transformed patrimonial individualism has come to dominate based on the notion of a sovereign postpatrimonial self who holds onto the ideal of self-government not in terms of collectivist self-rule but as separatist self-sufficiency. Similar to but qualitatively different from the patrimonial individual who claims jurisdiction and the right to rule over a dominion defined by private property, the postpatrimonial sovereign individual achieves subjectivity through its sovereignty over capital assets. Yeatman claims 'Whether an individualism of the self-sufficient will is to prevail or a more inclusive individualism can be established as the mode of subjective being is in question' (Yeatman, 2007, pp. 58–9).

In an article published in 2013 I reflected upon the potential of England's new free school policy to serve the interests of democracy and social justice (Boyask, 2013). The policy which allows for new academy schools to be established through interest group demand, regardless initially of school place needs, means that in reality they are likely to be similar in many respects to other self-governing schools, make an even bigger contribution to social segregation than other academy schools and therefore struggle to contribute to social justice. However, my analysis of their potential contribution to democracy was founded in conceptualizing their special status as an expression of collectivist or co-operative individualism. As Yeatman (2007) does in her discussion of contested individualisms, I drew on Durkheim's notion of two types of societal cohesion. In his 1893 work *De la division du travail social/The Division of Labour in Society* he identifies two mechanisms that may hold together a society. The first is mechanical solidarity, which attaches the individual to the group through repressive law and regulation and presumes that individuals within a society resemble one another. The second, which Durkheim terms organic solidarity, holds together a complex and differentiated society. Organic solidarity is dependent upon the difference of individuals in respect of their personalities and roles, and

> that the collective conscience leave open a part of the individual conscience in order that special functions may be established there, functions which it cannot regulate. The more this region is extended, the stronger is the cohesion which results from this solidarity. (Durkheim, [1893] 1984, p. 131)

Dewey's (1927) scepticism of the quality of public opinion in his era, and his perception that individuals had been divorced from the public sphere through technological and social complexity suggests that not all complex societies that exhibit specialization are founded on equal and reciprocal social relations. Yet there are similarities between the individualism in Durkheim's notion of organic solidarity and the co-operative individualism of Dewey. My argument regarding free schools was that their democratic potential lay in their conceptualization as sites that promoted differentiation through co-operative individualism within them and as differentiated from other institutions yet profoundly connected to them (Boyask, 2013). While this argument made no claims to anything other than potential democracy, others have also asked whether different forms of self-governing schools offer possibilities for democratic social relations.

In her paper 'Charter Schooling and Social Justice' Knight Abowitz (2001) drew upon Fraser's conceptualizations of multiple and polyvocal publics to develop a critical and controversial rationale for American charter schools.

> These multiple publics should be participants in larger publics but should also have the legitimate authority to form their own informal groups as well as formalized institutions. This is where the democratic possibilities for charter schooling enter the scene. (Knight Abowitz, 2001, p. 159)

The question she raises as to whether charter schools, under certain conditions, might be used to redistribute the good of education to marginalized groups to further social justice is provocative. In literature on privatization and choice in education, charter schools are typically regarded as tools of democratic capitalism (Wells et al., 2002). They promise entrepreneurial innovation and inventiveness, yet according to Lubienski (2009) their innovations are largely confined to practices of privatized organization and governance rather than innovations in educational method. From research on student attainment in seven states Zimmer et al. (2012) claim that there is no overall evidence of charter schools improving student achievement. While American charter schools differ from the privatized schools in English schooling, that is, academy and free schools, the underlying debate about what is in the public interest is increasingly relevant.

As my own research on privatized schools and schools within the private sector shows (Boyask, 2013; 2015b; 2018), some schools resist the competitive relations of a schooling market. These sites are important because they provide real-life laboratories in which we can observe tensions and conflicts that emerge as schools have to negotiate the influences of pluralist public opinion and accountabilities to multiple publics.

In the remainder of this chapter I draw on research introduced in Chapter 1 in Sands, a democratic privately funded secondary school in England, as a case study of the dynamics at work within a school that has its own character and values yet is inevitably connected to the wider social milieu. The case uses tools of analysis from Bernstein's (2003) work on social control and cultural transmission, including the classification and framing of curriculum and weak and strong pedagogy. These analytical tools highlight the individualisms and collectivity that develops through the school's internal and external relationships. Bernstein is relevant here because of his application of Durkheim's notions of mechanical and organic solidarity to describe the functioning of different kinds of schools. Bernstein built upon Durkheim's notions of mechanical and organic solidarity to describe different forms of schooling. His analysis of solidarity was more subtle than Durkheim's by taking into account differences in social structure between the fields of economy and culture, and historical change in respect of the middle class and its relationship to both fields (Bernstein, 2003; 2001). However, what he sought to highlight is that 'closed' schooling is characterized by overt mechanical solidarity and corresponds to traditional schooling with strong disciplinary boundaries and explicit regulation through curriculum, pedagogy and assessment. In contrast 'open' schooling has weakened classification and framing and uses implicit forms of symbolic control exercised through invisible pedagogy (Bernstein, 2003; Atkinson, 1985).

Bernstein associates open schooling with the parental pedagogies (in particular the maternal pedagogies) of a fraction of what he terms the new middle class and uses the analysis of its practices as a means to classify agents of symbolic control. In other words what appears to be liberatory and empowering schooling is the expression of a category of difference and one of privilege, which therefore strengthens social stratification. From a democratic perspective, however, the same weakened boundaries and invisible pedagogies can be understood differently, especially if the intent is as Dewey framed it, to make democratic discourses so prevalent and visible as to dominate in discourses of governance and thereby influence its practices.

Sands School is characterized by its location within the private sector, despite its significant differences from other private schools. The main difference of the school is its intention to blend private and participatory education through its democratic ethos, including through its practices of governance. It is the explicit intent of the school that its practices will support equality and participation; yet its situation within the private education sector excludes the possibility of free access, thus working against the school's values. It is put forward here as an example of a counterpublic that is forced into compromising its democratic values by the exercise of control of larger governmental structures, both through its regulation and the private school market.

The phenomenon under study was an attempt by the school to liberalize curriculum, with the curriculum, in Bernsteinian terms, shifting from a collection curriculum that was strongly framed, subject-based and largely set by accountability to national policy, to an apparently weakly framed integrated curriculum established by the interests of teachers and students at the school (Bernstein, 2003). While a Bernsteinian analysis of the curriculum reveals an underlying dynamic of educational transmission consistent with its classed location, the case is also explored for the extent and nature of transformative and participatory education (Dewey, 1916) to consider the wider implications for democratic participation within an environment of privatization. The case study provides an illustration of how one school manages its commitment to equality within private sector schooling, how individuals through the school's experiments in integrated curriculum enact their responsibilities in respect of the school's ethos and therefore live out their individualisms, and ultimately define the limits to the school's democracy.

The school

Sands School is a small privately funded secondary that in 2009 had a roll of sixty-eight students. Of the sixty-eight students, two had statements of special educational needs. There were forty girls and twenty-eight boys. It is in a rural, market town that is ranked in the lowest third for social deprivation, yet at the one state-funded secondary school in the town only 11 per cent of pupils claim free school meals compared with a national average of 15.9 per cent. Census returns from the local authority where the school is located showed considerably less ethnic diversity than other localities in England, and most of the students at Sands also identified as White British. Recent Ofsted (2010, 2013, 2016) inspections at Sands School report that it provides an education that is good with outstanding features, with particular recognition for outstanding provision in the spiritual, moral, social and cultural development of its students. The school describes its own philosophy on its website thus:

> We believe that everyone should be treated equally, be happy, and have access to good education. At Sands, no-one has more power than anyone else, the teachers and students are equal, and there is no headteacher. We try to get rid of all the petty rules, making room for everyone to be happy and free to express themselves in whatever way they feel. The school is democratic, with everyone having their say and equal vote in the weekly school meeting to which everyone may attend (and most do!). (Sands, 2010)

The school has been involved with an international network of schools known as the International Democratic Education Network (IDEN), which meet annually around the world to discuss and develop statements of common intent on their commitment to democratic principles. At the Berlin conference in 2005 the participants agreed on the following statement:

> We believe that, in any educational setting, young people have the right:
> - to decide individually how, when, what, where and with whom they learn
> - to have an equal share in the decision-making as to how their organisations – in particular their schools – are run, and which rules and sanctions, if any, are necessary. (IDEN, 2010)

It is this educational philosophy and the way that it is realized through the practices of the school that differentiates Sands from most schools within the private education sector. It is the intention at Sands that education starts with a basic premise of human equality. These values do of course conflict with the school's dependence upon private revenue, which means access to the education provided by the school is not equal because it is limited to students who can afford to attend. Most places are privately funded, and a small number funded by a charitable trust or by local authorities. Fees are below the national average for private school fees (Ryan and Sibieta, 2010). While there are many of the traditional professional roles at the school, such as teachers and teaching assistants, there is no head teacher. Governance at the school is generally conducted through a weekly school meeting where both students and teachers participate in decision-making around school administration and negotiate changes to policy and practice.

In comparison with some democratic schools the curriculum at Sands is conventional, adhering closely to the national curriculum to prepare students for the external examination GCSE generally taken in year 10 of schooling. The students follow a set timetable that is divided into discrete subjects such as mathematics, science, English, IT, art and so on. The research project at the school was a documentation and evaluation of curriculum innovation in the second half of the summer term in 2010. Some teachers at the school were dissatisfied with the traditional structure of the curriculum that appeared to foster students' compliance rather than the participation valued within the school ethos. Patrick, a teacher at the school, said during an interview:

> Both Daniel [the teacher leading the curriculum innovation project] and I believe that children should be active in their learning and this project lends itself towards children becoming more active. Even though we have this principle at the school that children work with a tutor and design their curriculum, which means that when they come to class, they have actively chosen to be in that class, very quickly an ordinary box timetable split up between subjects becomes just a timetable that the children feel that they ought to go to. I think you need to reinvent that a few times to remind the children that they are active participants in the school.

In the spirit of reinvention a short 'experiment' of four weeks was instituted where the timetable was abandoned and reverted to an open schedule timetable. During this period it was intended that students negotiated with teachers for them to either lead conventional classes and/or work on a range of interest-based projects. The structure of changes was explained to me by Daniel thus:

> Over a four week period, days will be organised into a series of sessions (probably one two hour slot before lunch and one after lunch each day) during which each member of the school will engage in an activity of their choice. Staff and students will be encouraged to run 'projects' that will have a specific goal for completion at the end of the four week period. Staff, in particular, will be encouraged to embed learning from areas of curriculum outside of their usual specialty into the project they devise, in order to explicitly show that knowledge and skills are not restricted to a particular area of learning.

The research project

To investigate the curriculum innovations we elected to use participatory research methods in keeping with the ethos of the school, involving students as researchers (Nairn and Smith, 2003). The involvement of student researchers was also in keeping with the nature of the proposed curriculum changes. Drawing upon Bernstein's conceptualization of weak and strong framing, Leat and Reid (2012) suggest that an integrated or process-orientated curriculum with weak subject boundaries is in general more responsive to student involvement than a strongly framed traditional, subject-based or 'collection' curriculum. A project team consisting of school and university researchers (i.e. two students and a teacher from the school; a research assistant and principal researcher from the university) designed and carried out an evaluation of the curriculum innovation. The school (through the school researchers and school meeting) selected three of the timetabled 'projects' for investigation, choosing a newspaper project, sound sculpture project and this evaluation (known as 'the research project') as a third project. The project team met once a week in a timetabled session to make decisions about research design and management. The university researchers provided guidance on research design, ethics, data analysis and dissemination, and the two student researchers undertook the majority of the field work. The main data collection was video recording undertaken by the student researchers. We discussed at one of the project team meetings how to capture teaching and learning on video. In addition to the video of the projects, the university researchers interviewed a sample of teachers, students and teaching assistants from the school, audio recorded project meetings, took field notes at school meetings and collected documentary evidence including a copy of the school newsletter, the school's Ofsted reports and video footage of the timetable (located on a board in the school grounds).

The school and university researchers worked in adherence with the Plymouth University ethics procedures and made use of the school's decision-making processes to negotiate ethical dilemmas. One of the main ethical considerations was the extent to which we could guarantee confidentiality. Given its rare democratic character it was recognized that entirely obscuring the school's identity would be difficult, so participants were informed that the school may be identifiable in publication, yet we would endeavour to obscure the identities of individuals. Individuals were given the opportunity to withdraw from the project, and this was a choice made by some. This was especially important with the collection of video data where individuals may not have control over whether they were captured in footage. The student researchers tried not to record individuals who had withdrawn and informed them that they might inadvertently be caught on video, in which case this footage would not be used in the analysis. Consequently, there were some individuals who participated in the case study projects, yet whose involvement is not considered in the analysis outlined in this chapter.

The video data were analysed using both deductive and inductive reasoning. First, the student researchers were asked to identify from the footage of the three projects a series of episodes where learning was taking place. Then the student researchers selected one exemplary episode from each project and discussed the rationale for their choice with the research assistant (this discussion was recorded and contributed to the analysis). They also provided a rich description of learning at Sands, so that evidence of learning from the video footage that they cited could be compared with this description. All of the selected footage and recordings of analysis was passed to me for inductive analysis, looking for patterns and points of significance that emerge from the video data and all the supplementary material (interview transcripts, documents, etc.). The primary insights that emerged from the data upon which I based my analysis were: (1) the interplay between the structured and structuring nature of curriculum, which was reproduced through patterned behaviours and expectations, and related to Bernstein's (2003) curricular types and invisible pedagogies; and (2) the progressive impulses for innovation and change, supported through legitimating new forms of participation, which has been related to Dewey's (1916) work on democracy and reconstruction of experience. This analysis was shared with the school, to highlight for them the implications of curricular change and what might inhibit its success. In the context of this book this analysis does different kinds of work. The liberalization of curriculum and weakening of its boundaries act as a context of societal dissolution and a Bernsteinian analysis suggests that the choices made by individuals are the forced choices theorized by Beck. Whereas a Deweyan perspective is more optimistic about the potential for individuals in this context to achieve subjecthood through participation, the curriculum of Sands provides a context in which a struggle between different individualisms can be seen.

Classification and framing within the projects

The nature of curriculum within the three case study projects differed, even while they were all situated within the wider agenda of an integrated curriculum within the open-schedule timetable. Basil Bernstein's concept of classification provides a lens to view the structure of curriculum in the projects. Classification 'does not refer to what is classified, but to the relationships between contents' (2003, p. 88). Using classification as a tool of analysis at the level of school curriculum should show up differences between the school's usual curriculum of disciplinary knowledge that has strong content boundaries compared with a new integrated curriculum with weakened content boundaries. An analysis of classification reveals its relative strength. So, for example, the newspaper project was focused upon the production of a newspaper, which gave momentum to the project and culminated in the production of a school newspaper entitled 'The Democrat'. The project departed from a clear subject-based curriculum and therefore was weakly classified by conventional disciplinary knowledge. In comparison, the sound sculpture project, which was intended to be interdisciplinary and encompass aspects of music, sound science and abstract art in practice, was taught in classes that were aligned with the usual timetable at Sands and classified by traditional subject divisions. This differed again within the research project that had weak content boundaries as its content was driven through the process of inquiry.

However, it is the framing of curriculum that is of most relevance to our discussion of public accountability. Framing of curriculum refers to the extent to which teachers and students have control over processes of 'selection, organisation and pacing of the knowledge transmitted and received in the pedagogical relationship' (Bernstein, 1971, p. 231). The newspaper project was organized organically, with weak framing and different participants taking on specialized roles in the project. The student researchers suggested that one of the best features of this project was that it was an initiative of one of the students (who they also suggested had a greater leadership role than the teaching assistant who also had oversight of the project). As the momentum for the project grew and it got closer to completion her leadership motivated more students to become involved. Content was discussed at regular editorial meetings, and leadership was distributed throughout numerous editorial roles. There were nineteen contributors overall. The weak framing of the project presented some difficulties. In some phases the contributors had limited knowledge of the processes needed to progress the newspaper. For example, while there was a large group who discussed and worked on design and layout of the paper in a classroom, this proved to be unwieldy so that ultimately the design decisions were made by a pair of students (including the project leader) working on a single computer in the computer lab.

The sound sculpture project was more traditionally taught in the sense that it was predominantly teacher initiated and led. The stronger framing of the project impacted considerably on the classification of the curriculum. While the connections between the disparate fields of investigation (i.e. science, art and music) were firmly in the minds of the project initiators, and therefore it might be assumed that the project had strong framing, there was little consistency in terms of which students took part in each of the sessions. A sound sculpture was manufactured, but its design was not clearly informed by the ideas explored in the session on abstract art, nor was it obvious how it reflected the ideas discussed about frequency and amplitude in the sound science session. The more successful aspects of this project were the experiences students had in the individual sessions. The student researchers selected part of a sound science session as their exemplary session, which they regarded as very successful because it showed teachers using anecdotes to explain scientific principles, students showing engagement through asking a lot of questions, teachers responding to their questions and allowing them freedom to follow their own lines of inquiry loosely bound by the topic under investigation. When talking about what she had observed here Jill, student researcher, said 'the students can direct where the learning goes, they can ask about what they're interested in and the teachers won't say "no, that's not what we're doing today"', suggesting this conversational approach typified how teaching and learning worked at Sands School. It differs from pedagogy generally enacted through schooling in England, as evidenced in the results of the PISA survey of 15-year-olds that finds students in England are more likely to be taught through traditional transmission models of teaching (OECD, n.d.). From my observation of the footage it seemed that this session and a similar art room session bore similarities to the usual practices of the school. It seems the conventional curriculum at Sands is dynamic because it is variously strongly classified by a discipline, yet through the weak framing conveyed through the school's pedagogy the curriculum is also weakly classified as students explore it from their own perspectives and experiences. This is an important point that will be returned to in the next section.

The research project differed from the other two projects because while decisions were made within the project team, which included school members, the overall oversight of the project came from outside the school through the university researchers. The project was intended to have a team of student researchers, but only two stayed involved in the project, and one of these attended many more project meetings than the other. Sara was new to the school and the project was significant in structuring her participation in the life of the school. She came to almost all meetings and took an active leadership role in the project, taking responsibility for keeping the research project going when the university researchers were not there. Sara began to act like a researcher through involvement in the project. She talked to the university researchers about her desire to document and understand what she saw. For example, she said:

> this is interesting how she or he is reacting to this, and you're thinking I should have a camera with me. But you don't have a camera with you because you have to keep putting it back. (Interview, 22 June 2010)

Jill was a senior student at Sands who was involved in many different activities in the school. She contributed to some meetings and the collecting of data, but involvement in the project appeared less significant to her than to Sara (although it should also be noted the project coincided with her GCSEs). The research project overall tended towards weak classification in relation to the school's subject-knowledge boundaries; however, towards the beginning of the project it was strongly framed by the researchers' knowledge of inquiry. Yet the framing changed as the student researchers became enculturated into the knowledge domain. By the middle of the project Sara was taking a significant role in directing the inquiry, weakening the strong framing of the project.

Participation and learning inside the projects

From a Bernsteinian perspective weak pedagogical framing within the case study projects is only apparently weak, and actually regulated through invisible pedagogy (Bernstein, 2003). For Bernstein invisible pedagogies in schooling emerged from an ideological conflict within the middle class between the strong classification and frames in the visible pedagogies of the public (in the English sense of elite private) schools and the weakly classified and framed invisible pedagogies of private schools for the new middle class (Bernstein, 2003; Arnot, 2002). Originating as a form of maternal control invisible pedagogies exert a more personal and implicit form of control than their visible counterparts; however, Bernstein (2001) speculated that it may be that weakly framed control is the most successful at social reproduction because its effects become habitual and taken-for-granted.

Bernstein's work is based upon classification and division, typical to his structuralist form of analysis, and he makes clear distinctions between the private or economic field, and the public or symbolic field (2001). Towards the end of his life in 2000 he recognized a change in the social order towards economic managerial control and 'the extension of market rationality' into the symbolic field, where he had previously located the teachers of state schooling as agents of symbolic control (Bernstein, 2001). The outcome of this economic interruption, and essentially centralized control of agents within the symbolic field was a 'totally pedagogized society' (p. 31). This is an important change when you consider Bernstein attributed responsibility to teachers for social reproduction within the symbolic field, thus their acts of invisible pedagogy assume immense significance in the reproduction of class fractions and maintenance of social inequalities.

Bernstein was concerned with education as a form of cultural transmission and social reproduction. On its own this presents a too pessimistic view of participation at Sands. While much of the case study data support a class-based analysis, there was evidence to suggest that practices at the school were not unvaryingly in the hands of the traditionally privileged, and that there may be other motivations at work among a school community that is not homogeneous. For example, a student successfully led the newspaper project; outsiders were invited to take on leading roles in evaluating the work of the school; and students in a science class directed a discussion that retained its strong disciplinary basis. These exceptions are important because they lead us towards viewing Sands not just as a venue of educational transmission but also a site that is polyvocal and educationally transformative. While Bernstein privatizes the school on the basis of its economic conditions, not to mention the knowledge that is produced there, Fraser (1990) claims that:

> efforts to 'privatise' economic issues and to cast them as off-limits with respect to state activity impede rather than promote the sort of free and full discussion that is built into the idea of a public sphere. It follows from these considerations that a sharp separation of (economic) civil society and the state is not a necessary condition for a well functioning public sphere. On the contrary ... it is precisely some sort of inter-imbrication of these institutions that is needed. (p. 74)

Waks (2010) suggests that like Fraser, Dewey regarded the recognition of difference as a force for revitalizing publics. While Bernstein perceives the interpolation of the economic within the symbolic field as an interruption that strengthens social divisions and exacerbates inequalities, for Dewey difference is the impetus for social change towards a more democratic and equal society. Furthermore, Waks suggests that revitalization of democracy comes from new association with outside groups that 'are potential sources of new civil society initiatives' (p. 675), perhaps from within schools that have developed as Fraser's counterpublics.

Whereas a Bernsteinian analysis reveals the reproductive nature of the curriculum projects, the same projects can be analysed from a participatory perspective. The addition of a Deweyan analysis gives scope to examine the motivations of participants that exist irrespective of class, for example, in recognition of forms of social organization that are based upon commonality and participation (significant in the democratic context of Sands) rather than the stratification and segregation implicit in a class analysis. Following Dewey's (1916) work on democracy and education, the type of participation engaged in by its members is integrally connected to the nature of the social group. A democratic group, with democracy the guiding principle of the school, can be characterized by the extent to which members have 'an equable opportunity to receive and to take from others' and a 'large variety of shared undertakings and experiences' (chap. 7, section 1, ¶5). In Table 6.1 framing or control is examined as a form of participation. Each of the projects is represented by an observation from the student researchers. The observations come from halfway through the duration of the curriculum innovation project.

The students' experiences within the projects show some qualities of democratic participation, although there was some variation in this within each of the case studies. While the timetable was intended to foster the diversity of stimulation required of Dewey's democratic society and widen opportunities for participation, in each case the intended new relationships competed with established habits of mind. This is evident in the way that wider participation was curtailed when the newspaper project reached an impasse in its participants' knowledge of design; the sound sculpture project engaged students in single and familiarly structured teacher-led art or science lessons, but had difficulties maintaining momentum in supporting active learning across disciplines; or that participation in the research project was greater for those who were least enculturated into the usual workings of the school (Sara and the university researchers). Fundamentally, this same dynamic we refer to when we claim that schools should regenerate society by encouraging participation in the reconstruction of knowledge (e.g. Dewey, 1916), yet are primarily intended to reproduce existing structures (e.g. disciplinary or institutional; Bourdieu and Passeron, 1990). The intention to be progressive paid off in some aspects of all the case study projects, yet it was the tendency to conservatism that proved the easier path to follow in constructing the curriculum of the sound sculpture project and when overcoming difficulties in the newspaper project, showing the

Table 6.1 Evidence of learning and the nature of participation

	Newspaper Project	Sound Sculpture Project	Research Project
Example of Learning	A large group of students of different year levels choose to participate in proof-reading activity. A student takes the main leadership role, with all others opting to take on different proof-reading tasks. Observation suggests a high level of engagement and focus, and their effort contributes towards the production of the newspaper.	A science session in the music room led by the science teacher who demonstrates scientific principles and engages students in conversation. The students are active in the conversation by asking questions. Their effort makes little contribution to the rest of the project because few of the students here are involved in the project's final outcome.	One of the student researchers says that she now looks at familiar situations with the eyes of a researcher and finds new significance in the conversations she has at the school. She is responsible for choosing what data to record on video. This work has significant effect on the outcomes of the project.
Nature of participation	• Power is distributed among a relatively wide group of participants in respect of defining content from the outset of the project. • Students frame each other's and their own processes of inquiry. • Individuals work towards the collective good of producing a newspaper.	• Power was in the hands of the teachers to strongly classify to familiar curricular territories (e.g. art, science). • Power distributed to students through engagement in processes of inquiry in this session, but not between sessions. • Individuals co-construct knowledge within the session, but there is little connection to the outcomes of the ongoing project.	• Content defined by the researchers, initially just the university researchers but increasingly student researchers as project evolves. • Power distributed from university to student researchers, as students become enculturated into the knowledge domain. • Greater intersubjectivity between university and student researchers as students become more knowledgeable.

challenges of working against processes of normalization even within a school that views itself as highly democratic and participatory.

Democratic participation in education markets

Bernstein (2001) recognized a social transformation occurring that was driven by market rationality as the state retreated from the economic field and directed agents from the economic field to take over management of the field of symbolic control. This transformation was also witnessed by Brown (1990) who described a shift in the twentieth century from schooling governed by meritocracy (the ability and effort of the pupil), to parentocracy, where schools are governed through deployment of the social and financial capital of parents. While a schooling system of meritocracy opened opportunities for some otherwise disadvantaged students, it was still a system of inequalities because it excluded others (ibid.). A parentocratic system is even less concerned with equitable redistribution of education and will inevitably support social divisions and inequalities, with its goal of cementing financial and intellectual resources within particular families. Parentocratic policies of parental school choice have seen supplier/consumer-type relationships come to pervade mainstream schooling (Gewirtz et al., 1995). Thus the social transformation witnessed by Bernstein was one of increasing social inequality, and this observation is now widely recognized not just by academics but also by world leaders and supranational organizations (OECD, 2011a; Giles, 2014). In any contemporary discussion of democracy and the public sphere it is important to consider the pervasive influence of market rationality. While Fraser (1990) has reconceptualized the public sphere as a location of multiple publics, and her thinking has been extended as a theoretical justification for new forms of public schooling (Knight Abowitz, 2001; Waks, 2010), it must be recognized that actual alternative democratic publics compete for discursive space with other social groupings (Wilson, 2010). There is no reason to expect that any group setting up a privately funded or semi-autonomous state-funded school (like charter and free schools) is driven by a commitment to the good of the public, and may be acting in the interests of an impoverished communitarianism as associated with the expansion of economic rationality (Peters and Marshall, 1996).

In the case of private schooling, democratic schools are competing with other schools (both state and privately funded) for students and must viably operate within the same economic field as other privately funded schools.

The dominance of market values within Bourdieu's field of power means the struggle between economic and cultural values is likely to be seen even within a school like Sands founded in the educational values of a cultural elite rather than the market values of an economic elite. There was limited evidence from observing the curricular projects at Sands that participation in the curriculum was significantly influenced through the school's situation within an education market. Data from the projects suggest they were influenced by educational philosophies and beliefs about educational practices, rather than economic concerns. However, there were data from Sands outside of the individual curricular case studies but within the wider context of curriculum reform at the school that suggested non-participation in the projects may have been influenced by a market view of schooling.

The school researchers (both students and teacher) and others from the school who were interviewed identified tensions arising from changing the timetable. In particular, prior to the timetable change and throughout its duration there was discussion among students, staff and a few queries from parents on how the changes would impact upon revision and preparation for GCSE. Once raised as a concern by students at the weekly school meeting, because of the importance placed upon this venue for decision-making, it became an issue that required negotiation and resolution. It even delayed the start of the project. Speaking about the extent of the concerns and how it was resolved so that the timetable changes could take place, Patrick, a teacher, told us:

> The hard thing is that the older children are more vocal, the younger children would generally be less vocal about their anxieties unless you create an intimate environment for them to do it. So what you get in fact is the impression that the GCSE group are anxious and the rest of the school is okay with it, but the truth is that lots of children across the ages and some staff are anxious but prepared to give it a go, as long as certain things were satisfied. For example, that certain things were built into the structure, some things were unmoveable, revision slots or set Maths times – things like that. (Interview, Friday, 11 June 2010)

These changes appeared to satisfy the majority, and the restructured timetable went ahead. However, other challenges emerged for some students. The biggest problem highlighted within project team discussions was that there were a number of students who were not participating at all or very little within the scheduled projects. While it is the policy of the school that classes are not compulsory, they find that overall attendance is usually very good and students go to class even though they are not compelled to do so. This can take time to become habitual for some students new to the school, but since attendance is the normal practice of their peers and classes are generally enjoyable, students become acculturated into attending. Daniel, the teacher researcher in the project team, found that he was surprised by how much some students were struggling with the new timetable, to the extent where they were not engaging with it.

Aiden was a student identified during a project team meeting as struggling with the new timetable structure and was also noticed by a university researcher at a school meeting. The researcher noted in her field notes that Aiden challenged the teachers by questioning the educational content of the project-based curriculum and its teaching, complaining that 'you guys are paid for teaching this ... We need more info [like] the subject you are learning and a description of what you will be doing' (field notes, 16 June 2010). At a project team meeting we discussed the case of Jacob, who had been at the school for two years. Daniel said that Jacob had originally struggled with the different expectations compared with his previous school and did not attend classes. While Jacob had now turned that around, Daniel recognized that a new timetable that required more self-direction might be particularly challenging for him. Jacob discussed difficulties he was having with the new timetable at the same school meeting where Aiden had also commented. Jacob liked the old timetable because 'you could look at it and see that's what you've got' and he 'didn't like running around trying to organise it' (field notes, 16 June 2010). Daniel reflected that Jacob's difficulties with a changed schedule were precisely the kind of problems that he had hoped the new timetable would address. The curriculum innovations were intended to make students more actively involved in their learning, so that 'it is that reconstruction or reorganization of experience which adds to the meaning of experience, and which increases ability to direct the course of subsequent experience' (Dewey, 1916, chap. 6, section 3, ¶2). To varying extents, the students who participated in the case study projects were engaged in reconstructive or progressive learning. Their participation tended towards conservatism or normality when faced with a challenge to their ability to direct their own experiences, either due to complexity of the task or through limited understanding of what was required of them; however, Jacob and Aiden and the others who did not participate in the projects were not accessing the intended curriculum. They had the ability to pay for access but did not recognize the experiences offered as educational and responded with resistance and direct challenges to the teachers. Importantly, Aiden justified this response by drawing attention to the economic relationship between the student consumers and the teachers who are the service providers of the school.

While it is problematic to wholly attribute to market rationality the resistances to transformative education seen within the school, they do mesh with commercial interests. Jacob and Aiden act as the sovereign individuals of neoliberalism to exercise their rights as consumers of education (Davies and Bansel, 2007; Yeatman, 2007). The resistance to curricular changes by students concerned about their effect on GCSE preparation embody middle-class capital accumulation and positioning within a market economy. These resistances are also interesting to consider in respect of the school's relationship with the state, particularly the case of exam preparation since it is through the school's decision to offer a GCSE programme that it is most securely tied to the state. When Habermas (1991) developed his theorization of the public sphere as a site of critical dialogue and debate, he located it outside of both state and economy. With a shift from producer to consumer culture the public sphere transforms from a site of deliberation and decision-making to become a site of display and superficiality. It is unsurprising that at points where the school is most closely coupled with the economy that it least resembles a democratic public. But it is also the case that at points where the school is most closely coupled with the state the school tends away from democratic participation and equality. While Fraser (1990) argues for inter-imbrications between state and economy in the formation of strong publics, it is the state's imbrication with the economy which restricts a democratic curriculum at Sands School. This is not to argue for separating schools from the state, indeed Dewey (1915) suggests it is necessary to conceive of schools as seamlessly connected with broader society, but to highlight that the quality of the public within schools is affected by wider ideologies of state. By implication we must be very careful not to exclude from public debate examples of democracy in the private schooling sector, when we are at risk of losing all state-funded instantiations of democratic schooling to manifestations of the neoliberal state.

Public accountability in a conditional counterpublic

What does the case of Sands show us about public accountability and the challenge of realizing the public good within pluralist publics? The combination in Sands of its commitment to equality and location outside of the mainstream public sphere provides a window onto the world of a counterpublic. Democracy is embedded within its governance even though the extent of its democracy is limited, as private school fees restrict who participates in its democracy. In this sense its governing public provides a good illustration of how a conditional counterpublic makes governmental decisions based both upon its own philosophies of practice and those of stronger, larger and influential public spheres. Conceiving publics as pluralist means that social action is shaped by pluralist public opinions, and social agents are subject to or held account to different opinions on what counts as the public good. Within Sands can be seen struggles between the school's own internal drivers and its external influences such as the strong curricular framing within some of the projects, student and parental expectations around national examinations and even the market discourses that emerged in resistance to the curriculum innovation. Discourse within the school is framed in respect of the school's relationship to the state and the market, or in this case the inter-imbrication between both state and market.

Public accountability of the individual to the state is hidden in neoliberalism, even though its functioning is actually dependent on the exercise of its control over the individual. While the individuals conceived in a neoliberal state are only apparently sovereign, individualization dominates the contemporary social imaginary. Yet as Yeatman (2007) points out there is a struggle at work within the individualization of society between a discredited patrimonial sovereign individual and a collectivist, subjective individual. The Bernsteinian analysis of the pedagogic discourses that frame the individuals at Sands highlights the reproductive qualities within the curriculum innovation. That is, despite a desire for release the individuals are held accountable by traditional pedagogic framing or they are only apparently free to participate as sovereign individuals in an educational market. The demands of the students who resisted participation in the projects might be framed as holding the school to account, but it is accountability to their needs as individual consumers rather than a collective good. This is an impoverished notion of accountability.

What interests me most about the school is the persistence and perhaps stronger influence on its individuals of creative and productive forces of mutuality and reciprocity. The majority of students were engaged in the projects, and the most successful projects were developed in respect for the school's philosophy that encourages participation in opinion formation and decision-making for the good of all. Within the three projects there are examples of struggles between traditional and progressive pedagogies. From a Bernsteinian perspective that focuses on the reproduction of social strata, both of these pedagogies exemplify control in the hands of the teacher; the control in traditional pedagogies is explicit, whereas the weakened framing of progressive pedagogy is an implicit control. However, weakened framing can also be read as a redistribution of control. From a democratic perspective including students in decision-making is recognition of their subjectivity and rights of participation. In each of the projects there are examples of how student subjectivity contributes towards the good of the group. Rather than dismiss their participation and decision-making as forced choices, it can be framed as inclusion and responsibility to the collective. This reading is not unproblematic. As a counterpublic Sands is not accountable to mainstream publics through its democracy, only through its consumption value. Unlike ideal publics Sands is forced into a compromise of conditional equality as it negotiates a position in respect of both economy and state. In Sands' curriculum innovation, participation within the projects represents a form of direct democracy that is the intended agenda of the school. Here we have a small group of students participating in a localized democracy within a very small school that has only a marginal relationship with democratic processes of state. Strengthening publicness within Sands would require the extension of its democratic processes outside of the school, and that would require that individuals within the school regard themselves as held to account by larger, external democratic publics.

7

Bounded Public Service

The previous chapter examined public accountability within the context of a conditional counterpublic, or alternative public sphere that formed within the private school Sands. This chapter expands on the theme of public accountability and extends it to consider how responsibilities to the public are enacted through public service within a context of practical politics. The notion of public service in this chapter is examined within a much more conventionally public context, by examining the accountability of geographically bounded local authorities to their decision-making publics. The local authorities in England consist of democratically elected Councils and administrative divisions and, increasingly, arm's-length business units. Local authorities are at the centre of interesting interrelationships between state, market and public. While they form part of the state their mandate means they are accountable to their local community and not to parliament (MHC&LG, 2018). Their devolved responsibility includes the capacity to raise their own taxes, and while central government grants constitute a larger share of their funding than local sources, the balance has been shifting towards locally funded income since central government funding cuts in 2010. Reduction in funding has forced local authorities to find new ways to generate income to meet their statutory responsibilities, and as the research reported in this chapter shows, the answer has been to embrace some form of privatization for some or most of their services. Educational services in local authorities are especially at risk from privatization because education has and still does represent the biggest category of expenditure for local authorities. Local authorities have not only seen cuts to central government bulk funding grants, they have also lost revenue through the academies policy that sees school grants go directly to the schools themselves whereas previously the monies came through them.

In Chapters 3 and 4 I introduced a research project where I undertook four case studies of local authorities and the approaches they had taken to privatization. My intention in these earlier chapters was to highlight the co-operative values of one of the local authorities to show its commitment to social equality even though the authority operated and engaged with a context of competition. The co-operative local authority had attempted a compromise between the economic ambitions for local government set by the central government and the values of the local co-operative council: democracy, responsibility, fairness and partnership. The compromise results in contestations between the ideals of the council and their financial reality, not just impacting upon the way that public service is able to be enacted but also by transforming the public servants' own views of their roles.

> If somebody had told me a couple of years ago that I would be sitting down having conversations about what we are going to charge schools on a daily basis, what our costings are going to be, what we are going to charge for a twilight session and how we are going to market this? Because I have no marketing team in my department; it's what we do, and it is learning as you go along. But if somebody had said that to me a couple of years ago, I would have said, 'No, that's not going to happen.' So, the commercial aspect of it has been a real challenge and still is and it has been a steep learning curve and the team I think is still adjusting to that. If we don't sell our services people will lose their jobs. (Interview, 10 April 2013)

As funding cuts strike deeper, it is realized by the head of children services that the traded service offer will need further restructuring; she proposes that it is removed from the local authority's direct control and set up as a private business. Yet the local authority is still unwilling to eschew entirely its co-operative values and looks to establish a mutual or community interest company in partnership with other educational enterprises already established within the city.

The current public policy context is one dominated by market relations (Robertson and Dale, 2013). In response to the global economic crisis the overall climate in England has been one of austerity, restricting the role of government; yet the limits placed on government do not have solely practical origins but are also driven by ideology (Robertson et al., 2012; Mazzucato, 2013). Social goals take second place to economic goals, and the state's response to its social responsibilities is shaped by free market and autonomous individualistic ideologies. In England we saw funding taken away from local authorities who had a substantial responsibility for schooling, and policy reform that reallocated it to schools so they may choose where they purchase services. The study of local authorities set out to understand how local authorities within the south-west of England responded to changes in legislation and associated funding cuts.

Yet, my main finding from the study was that while the solution to the external circumstances had in each case led to a similar solution, that is, privatization, the motivations and values underpinning them were in each case different. In other words, they each represent a different view of the role of a local authority and its approach to public service. While social equality is more obviously stated in the principles of the co-operative Council, social goals are also motivators for the other local authorities. However, they have different concepts of the social, who constitutes the public and the role of the local authority. These differing conceptualizations meant that the local authorities conceptualized and acted in the public interest differently in respect of their work with schools.

The changes seen within these local authorities are consistent with wider movements in privatization, a process that has many contested meanings but, in education, is commonly explained as withdrawal of the state from public provision and movement towards private or market-based provision (Starr, 1988; Robertson et al., 2012; Wilson, 2012). However, as discussed in earlier chapters privatization viewed in this way conflates public with the state and private with market, and is an analysis that is too heavy-handed. The research presented in this chapter demonstrates private interests are subtly different things within different local authorities. It is also too simplistic to bracket off the private sphere from the public. Even the term 'privatization' suggests a relationship between public and private, and within an environment of privatization local authorities retain statutory responsibility for overseeing the performance of schools and holding them to account for upholding the public interest.

For children and young people the main statutory duties of local authorities include: ensuring there is fair access to schooling; supporting vulnerable children; improving the performance of schools and ensuring high standards; using their democratic mandate to advocate for parents, families and children (DfE, 2010b; Parish, Baxter and Sandals, 2012). While these responsibilities are largely of a social order, the dominance of economic relations within the public policy environment limits the extent of the agency of local authorities in fulfilling these duties. This dominance also shapes how local authorities and others interpret their responsibilities. Diminishing budgets work against aspirations for socially democratic forms of inclusion, meshing more readily with the social and economic aspirations of human capital. A typical example of human capital comes from a recent report from the London School of Economics Growth Commission (Aghion et al., 2013) which focuses upon the needs of disadvantaged pupils, not for humane reasons but because

Our failure to provide adequate education to children from disadvantaged backgrounds constitutes a waste of human resources on a grand scale. It holds back economic opportunities and is detrimental to growth. (17)

Human capital theory forms the dominant view of public services and regards government as a safety net against market failure. While in the new environment local authorities retain statutory responsibility for all children and young people, in the reported research they claimed that their primary responsibility was to the most vulnerable. However, each of the local authorities had a different orientation to their role and there are important qualitative differences in their models of service.

The south-west region of England is an interesting context in which to observe local authorities because a significant number of schools have embraced recent reforms of schooling. In response to the Liberal Democrat/Conservative government's invitation for all schools to join the academy programme, twenty-seven schools in Cornwall and forty schools in Devon by July 2010 had expressed interest in converting to academies (Rogers, 2010). This compared with a national average of thirteen schools per local authority. By mid-2014, a total of 593 academy schools had opened in the south-west England region, taking the funding from the local authorities and placing it in the hands of individual schools. As well as financial loss as a result of schools converting to academies, in the four years from 2011 local authorities are subject to funding cuts to their formula grants, amounting to a national average cut of 27 per cent (Stabe and Jones, 2011).

This research study presented here identifies and analyses four different models of service adopted by local authorities in this region as a result of these changes. I term the four models: co-operative; entrepreneurial; community engagement; and corporate. Each is underpinned by different beliefs about the role of local authorities and the public–private relationships through which they carry out their work. Key informants from the four local authorities were questioned about the values and practices of their organizations. The study also surveyed schools, asking whether they considered that the values and principles underpinning the local authorities' models of service aligned with the work of their school. Economic relationships are found to be a major influence in the different models of service and the new models of service can all be characterized as forms of the enactment of privatization. The remainder of this chapter begins with a brief description of the research project and then outlines each model, considering qualitative differences between the models of service and the significance different forms of privatization have for public service in a highly competitive and resource-limited social environment.

Relations between local authorities and schools

The study focused on four local authorities selected because they were quite different in terms of their demography, geography and constituencies. LA1 is a large borough authority; LA2 is a small, non-metropolitan authority; LA3 is a large unitary county authority; and LA4 is a unitary authority in an average sized city (Table 7.1).

The local authorities were also selected because, through a preliminary review, it was apparent that they each responded differently to the changes in policy. Data collection included: (1) a review of publicly available documentary evidence on the interface between the local authorities and schools (including traded services and joint ventures) that included minutes of meetings, catalogues of services, media reports, newsletters, policy documents, action plans, inspection reports and others; (2) interviews with eleven senior managers and service providers (although notably only one participant from LA2 agreed to be interviewed); and (3) a survey of state-funded primary and secondary school service users in the local authorities that had an overall response rate of 14 per cent. Data were collected in 2012–13.

These data were supplemented by demographic data from government statistics (e.g. 2011 census and 2010 multiple deprivation indices). Further data were provided by interview respondents, who in some cases supplied policy documents, pamphlets and other internal publications. The project was granted ethical approval at Plymouth University. The research questions address professional and commercial ethics, and to encourage open responses respondents were assured that as far as possible all reports of the research would keep their involvement confidential.

Table 7.1 Case studies: The local authorities

LA1	LA2	LA3	LA4
Shire County	Non-metropolitan Unitary	Unitary, County	Unitary, City
Conservative controlled	Conservative controlled	No overall control (majority Libdem, Ind and Con)	Labour controlled
Population 746,400	Population 131,000	Population 532,300	Population 256,400
457 schools	58 schools	332 schools	108 schools

The data were analysed deductively, using content analysis to draw out findings that relate to the established research questions. This is interpretive research that draws conclusions through interpreting the research findings and relating them with existing knowledge of the privatization of state services.

Models of service

The four local authorities within this study have made profound structural changes to how they relate with schools. This has mainly meant following a path of privatization with models of service based upon local authorities commissioning services from other providers, their own traded offer (local authority-based services offered at a cost) or a combination of both, in order to meet their statutory responsibility to the public interest. However, the four local authorities have each responded in subtly different ways to the new policy and funding environment, entering into different kinds of public–private partnerships with different types of private actors (see Table 7.1). The models of service within each of these local authorities are all similar in that they represent a retreat from public provision, yet there are qualitative differences in how they orientate themselves towards the market and dominant discourses of good government (Table 7.2).

The economic theory most influential in current government reform is based on distinctive views of the state and market. In this view the market, classified with private interests, is a vehicle for innovation; the state's role in protecting the public interest is to respond in the exceptional circumstance of the market's failure to provide for all interests, thus acting as a safety net for society's most vulnerable (Robertson et al., 2012; Mazzucato, 2013). This implies that local

Table 7.2 Models of service: Local authorities

LA1 Corporate	LA2 Community Engagement	LA3 Entrepreneurial	LA4 Co-operative
A fully corporate model, developing a joint venture with a multinational corporation.	Community and stakeholder engagement, commissioning services from schools.	A small statutory provision (although under threat of closure), and an entrepreneurial business unit.	Aspirations for co-operative models of business, following the lead of their Council.

authorities take a minimal role in service provision yet retain the capacity to intervene when private provision fails. Of the four case studies, LA1 and LA2 were the most pared down in respect of services and local authority personnel. Respondents in each of these local authorities indicated that their core function was strategic oversight of services rather than provision. Yet it was only respondents from LA1 who expressed a particular commitment to the market as provider.

Corporate model

In LA1, the main partnership is through a joint venture between the local authority and a FTSE 100 Index company. The view expressed by commissioners and providers from this local authority is that schools should have control over their own purchasing power. The joint venture must compete for their custom alongside other providers, which, it is argued, will drive up the quality of the service. The core work of the joint venture includes school improvement services, learner services (including educational psychology and special educational needs, SEN) and school support services paid for from the local authority's £10.5 million commissioning pot. The local authority only provides directly admission and some transport services. The local authority's commissions from the joint venture fulfil its statutory responsibility to schools, children, young people and their families, and focus particularly upon 'vulnerable kids' (LA1, Interview, 11 April 2013). However, it is expected that the traded service will grow beyond the local authority's limited commissioning of statutory service, and the joint venture increase its income through selling services directly to schools. Talking about the relationship between the local authority and joint venture, a senior manager from LA1 said:

> So, we commission on behalf of some schools and we provide in a sense a trading platform; and then they go out and trade with those schools who are buying extra educational psychology beyond our statutory function; they're buying additional welfare services; they're buying additional support around school improvement if they need it. (LA1, Interview, 11 April 2013)

LA1 is a manifestation of 'new contractualism' in local government that separates policy making from policy delivery and potentially weakens the 'traditional values of public service, personal responsibility, and professionalism' (Curtis, 2008, p. 282). A contractualist interpretation of public service means social obligation is mediated by individualized consent within contractual arrangements (Yeatman, 1996), making individuals who lack the capacity to make choices for their own advantage vulnerable to injustice. LA1's attempt to meld its responsibility to the public interest with contradictory corporate values of competition, efficiency and profitability has the capacity to generate considerable tension between its business and social goals. Senior managers within LA1 recognize difficulties of attending to social need in the new policy and financial context, especially at a time when global uncertainties are increasing social inequalities (OECD, 2011a; Giles, 2014). It is further evident this local authority has faced challenges to the way it addresses its statutory responsibilities. Public debate and protests over LA1's privatization agenda reported in the media and a recent Ofsted inspection report have been highly critical of some aspects of the work of LA1.[1]

Community engagement model

LA2 has also considerably reduced its service provision and no longer directly provides school improvement services, yet unlike LA1 it retains some provision for the most vulnerable children rather than commissioning all of those services. It is also considerably different from LA1 in the types of private actors with whom it established partnerships. The main partnerships of LA2 are with local schools and school leaders, having contracted school personnel to the local authority just prior to the 2010 change of government.

> The director of Children's Services in about early 2010 took the view that it would be useful to have heads working and paid to work part-time within the local authority, to build that bridge between the schools and the local authority … .
> And so we had a primary head of school leadership and a secondary head of school leadership.
>
> And through those two heads working initially two and a half days a week for the local authority and then two and a half days a week back in their schools we started to develop this journey. (LA2, Interview, 10 April 2013)

As the service model moved from provider to commissioning agency, the local authority maintained the relationship through short-term contracts with these and other heads and 'expert' teachers in the region. More recently they have developed close relationships with their primary teaching school to deliver school improvement services. There are limited empirical data from LA2, with most publicly available documentation predating the reforms and only one interviewee; however, the model presented to me was one that emphasized partnership between the local authority and schools, helping to build community among schools and encouraging schools to work together with the teaching school acting as a hub for joint practice development, research and development, leadership and initial teacher education (LA2 pamphlet, n.d.).

The discourse of partnership is a common feature of recent public policy, identified by Ball and Exley (2012) as a demonstration of network governance that promotes a utopian vision where 'mutual respect, equal power and shared goals between parties are presupposed and disciplinary and other differences are elided over in an organizing structure which emphasizes "community"' (Frankham cited in Ball and Exley, 2012). In other words, while the interviewee emphasized partnership and community in describing LA2's model of service, hierarchies and competition were evidently built into the model with only some schools and individuals granted status as 'experts' and 'improvers' by organizations like Ofsted and National College, and these statuses rewarded financially through commissions from the local authority. Further research is required to better understand how power and participation operate within a community engagement model, and the extent to which the relationships within this environment are mutual ones.

Entrepreneurial model

At the time of data collection two local authorities, LA3 and LA4, had retained service units within the local authority, shifting the majority of service to a traded rather than statutory offer. These units were at arm's length from the core work of the local authority, and to different degrees they were expected to function independently and generate income. Indeed, in LA3 staff were contracted on commission rather than paid a salary, which is a practice intended to encourage their innovation. Mazzucato (2013) suggests an alternative to conceptualizing the role of the state as a safety net is to conceive of the state as a confident, innovating and entrepreneurial force for driving economic growth that will benefit all. An entrepreneurial state drives innovation and the profits that are returned from this innovation are ploughed back into public services to serve the common good (Mazzucato, 2013). The will for an entrepreneurial state is most evident in LA3, a local authority that attempted to blend social and economic goals through an entrepreneurial approach to public service. While this local authority retained a small unit for the provision of statutory school improvement services, it had embraced an entrepreneurial model for its main traded service unit. Their service model is driven by both economic and social values, apparent in the following extracts from their statement of *Vision, Values and Principles*:

> We ensure efficiency and value support the quality of our services.
>
> Research and cutting edge practice support innovation in our services and products.
>
> We value and respect all.
>
> We value the abilities of all our learners and encourage them to develop their potential. (LA3 pamphlet, n.d.)

LA3's traded service unit drives new projects and seeks new sources of revenue, including initiatives and products that they market beyond the region. It trades a catalogue of services to schools within its region, and also to schools in other authorities. It also works beyond its regional boundaries through offering services to other local authorities and through the development and marketing of educational products, such as literacy resources. However, innovation within the authority is not unrestrained, and the traded service unit is in some respects restricted in its activities by what schools want, can afford and are prepared to pay for. The authority must also respond to directives from central government on curriculum and assessment as well as other elements of the local authority's statutory duties so resources are also directed towards a school improvement service unit that is not part of its trading arm. Furthermore, because the unit remains attached to the council it is not fully resourced for enterprise: for example, it has no internal marketing or sales expertise. Despite a will for entrepreneurial government, strategic leaders in both LA3 and LA4 recognized that their current structures were unsustainable in the face of further funding cuts. Both local authorities were considering moving the traded service into stand-alone companies. For LA3 this would mean

> We'll have more flexibility around things like that [marketing and sales]; we can look seriously at whether it's worth having our own marketing and sales people. I would have thought with the nature of the changing landscape and the competition out there that would make real sense. (LA3, Interview, 4 April 2013)

Members of the service unit have struggled to fulfil the entrepreneurial promise of the unit, they claim, because it remains attached to the council and is not fully resourced for enterprise: for example, it has no internal marketing or sales expertise. The entrepreneurial local authority embraces business models for its services yet retains a commitment to equality expressed in its publicity as: 'we value the abilities of all our learners and encourage them to develop their potential' (pamphlet, n.d.). The chapter explores the extent to which this local authority's commitment to equality and the former local authority's commitment to co-operative values are sustained within the services provided.

Co-operative model

LA4 had also become a traded service, with a full catalogue produced and distributed among schools. Yet the local authority was concerned their provision was not sustainable and it was proposed that they establish a joint venture with one of the community interest companies already developed by schools in the locality or create their own joint venture company. The preferred corporate model for the proposed venture was a co-operative mutual, since this meshed with the council's commitment to co-operative values. Respondents from LA4 recognized that working co-operatively would be challenging, because the structural reforms had created a hostile and competitive environment among schools.

> And they [the schools] felt that they'd become very competitive, and I actually used the word to a couple of them that they'd become combative, because there were some quite unpleasant strands out there, and some non-collaborative behaviours. And a couple of Heads said to me, 'If you do nothing else but hold us together and point us in the direction, you'll absolutely have earned your salary'. (LA4, Interview, 2 April 2013)

While both LA3 and LA4 were operating traded service models, 75 per cent of school survey respondents perceived LA4's approach as close to their own values, compared with 53 per cent of school respondents from LA3. This may suggest LA4 has retained elements of a traditional notion of public service, as it is suggested by this head teacher:

> I believe that the same public service ethos that the local authority operates from is one that schools should also have. (LA4 Headteacher, survey response)

Alternatively, it might suggest the schools share with the local authority new entrepreneurial values rather than the co-operative values the local authority wishes to promote. Other comments from schools in LA4 highlighted that the local authority faced similar problems as the more business-orientated authorities, such as describing LA4 as 'occupied by self-survival', and noticing gaps in provision for even the most vulnerable schools (e.g. 'very little challenge and support available to those schools in a vulnerable position'). In current research and debate there is growing interest in the potential of mutuals and the co-operative movement for furthering social goals within a social context dominated by economic discourses (Webster et al., 2012), yet there is also evidence of large-scale market failure of co-operative models of business and governance (Kelly, 2014). Furthermore, this local authority is attempting to forge co-operative partnerships with schools fragmented through their location in a competitive economy of schooling where there are falling rolls and new market competitors (two new free schools and a University Technical College have recently opened).

Implications of reform across the local government sector

The local authorities reported in this study recognize their statutory responsibilities for disadvantaged children. However, recent structural reforms are impacting in various ways on their capacity to act upon these responsibilities. This research suggests that a market economy of schooling and services to schools impacts upon local authorities' capacity to meet the needs of disadvantaged children and young people. Local authorities need the financial and human resources to respond to the issues that come to them. As inequalities within society increase, there will be greater demand placed upon local authorities to respond to the needs of children. The reported study indicates that there remains a considerable lack of clarity around role and responsibility in the interactions between schools and local authorities and also through external relationships with governmental bodies such as Ofsted. While a simple solution to the ambiguity may appear to be more clearly defining lines of accountability, there is a deeper problem to be resolved. Current policies impacting upon the education and care of children emphasize competition, including the academies programme, forcing schools and local authorities to compete for custom. While three of the four case studies reported upon in this chapter are attempting to mitigate the competitive conditions, the evidence suggests that external pressures such as funding and central accountability are working against their attempts at cooperation or supporting community engagement.

Even though local authorities retain statutory responsibility for fairness in school access, school performance, vulnerable children and advocacy for children, parents and families, local authorities reported external perceptions that they are no longer responsible for schooling generally, and academy schools in particular. A local authority strategic manager within a considerably reduced core team after adopting a competitive market model of service reported that in spite of reform 'where I'm sitting it feels very much the same because all the issues and concerns, whether they're about academies or not, come into us'. This respondent also stressed the very important role local authorities need to play in taking responsibility for excluded and vulnerable children and young people. Yet this respondent also said:

> We've got two children [from an overseas country] found strapped to the bottom of a lorry ... And we've got a whole range of services now working, sorting those children out. They're in foster care, getting them into school, the right support services. They're very homesick; trying to make contact with their families. All that stuff is really important. **And we are doing it a bit on a shoestring I have to say at the moment.** (Interview, 11 April 2013, brackets and emphasis added by researcher)

An Ofsted report from a local authority inspection from the same region was released shortly after this interview, raising serious concerns about child protection services. It claimed that within the inspected local authority 'there are systemic weaknesses in managerial oversight and quality assurance that enable inconsistent and ineffective practice to go unchallenged and as a consequence some children and young people are exposed to unnecessary risk of significant harm'.[2] This was also a local authority that had adopted a fiercely competitive market model of services for children and young people, drawing upon the financial backing and commercial experience of a corporate partner. The more market-orientated local authority in my study adopted a position of broker between service providers and schools. The local authorities who have attempted to mitigate the effects of competition because it fragments cooperation among schools or works against the interests of the most disadvantaged remain located within market relations.

The solutions for survival within a market economy of services to schools for all the case study local authorities have been the disestablishment of provision within the local authority, and move towards commissioning models to fulfil statutory duties. Service provision as a core function of the local authorities is almost non-existent, and the traded services are offered to both maintained and academy schools. This leaves local authorities trying to account for differences in their commitments to maintained schools compared with academies. In many cases there remains little difference. Yet some local authority respondents argue there is a difference in quality of service between statutory and traded provision. A respondent who at the time of interview retained a position within a small statutory provision unit within a local authority under threat of becoming a fully traded service said:

> It's not a foregone conclusion that commissioning out and putting things to arm's length will diminish the service, but I think there is a fear that it could … Certainly in practical terms, I can see that if I and my colleagues are commissioned out, then a lot of the stuff that just lands on your desk on a day-to-day basis I'm really concerned about who will do that? If I'm commissioned to do specific things I will do those specific things, I will become a traded service. Who will pick up all the little incidental things which if they're not picked up sometimes become huge things. Personally I have fears about that, and I know that most of the colleagues I work closely with have fears about that as well … we are really genuinely worried about it in terms of the service that the schools, families and children will be receiving. (Interview, 16 May 2013)

Discussion

The four local authorities have each orientated themselves to the private sector differently as they respond to their statutory obligations, and attempt to distinguish themselves by forming partnerships with different kinds of private actors. The models adopted by the local authorities project different societal assumptions about the relationship between private and public interests, located upon a continuum of free market to mutual economics. These differences are related to the value bases of the local authorities and are also visible in the new relations they forge with schools. LA1's corporate model is centred on service delivery through its joint venture with a multinational company that was designed to expand its market share by catering to consumer demand. The local authority had only retained a very small core operation outside of the joint venture, and it is evident from both interviews and publicly accessible documents like inspection reports and news media that the local authority is struggling to meet its statutory duty, as critics of privatization would expect. LA3 had also embraced a market model, although the model observed during the data collection was an amalgamation of state and business, with the majority of its service delivery located in a trading business unit. This model differed from LA1 because rather than retreating from state involvement in delivery, it conceived of the state as an entrepreneurial force. However, almost half of the schools in LA3 thought the values of the local authority differed from those of their own. A headteacher whose school used LA3's school improvement services felt that the current provision did not meet demand, but suggested that pressures on the local authority were applied from outside.

> I believe they are being asked to do an almost impossible job re school improvement with limited resources and so many schools needing support due to the recent spate of Ofsted judgements. (LA3 Headteacher, survey response)

These external pressures account for LA3 and LA4's expected moves further away from provision and they are unlikely to lessen in the near future. Since the research, overall income has been declining in the sector from 2014/15 with increased local funding not matching the decline in government funding let alone inflationary costs, making the job of local authorities harder. While LA1 appears to be struggling to meet statutory responsibilities through its local authority-based strategic core and corporate model of traded service, there are similar tensions emerging for the other local authorities. Even within co-operative business structures governed by democratic principles, competitive market relations and centralized authority are fundamental features (Chaddad, 2012), opening up risks for market failure through competition and representing a further challenge for responding to social need. Correspondingly, LA2 has opted for a model of community engagement, yet even here the relations between school and local authority are fundamentally based upon an economic contractual relationship that challenges traditional notions of public service. In all these examples of privatized educational services the traditional practices of professionalism and public service have become enmeshed with practices of new contractualism and new public management to some extent.

While all the local authorities are seeking to uphold their responsibilities to the public interest through forms of privatization, the different models of service suggest they each are informed by subtly different sets of values. Schools suggest LA2 and LA4 are more closely aligned with their own values, and the values expressed by both these authorities also appear more closely aligned with community engagement and participation. Yet, even within these authorities the data show they share with the more business-orientated models similar tensions and challenges in fulfilling statutory duties. While social enterprises and co-operative models of business represent compromises between economic and social values, it is important to recognize that they are compromises and therefore these models of service are always open to the risks of market failure. Yet the market is not the only constraint upon service in the public interest. These new models of service are operating in a public policy context where public services are largely conceptualized as a safety net for those deemed to be most in need within a predefined group (Robertson et al., 2012; Mazzucato, 2013). The definition or prelegitimizing boundary of the group also acts to exclude and privilege interests. In both cases, when the new models of service fail, it is the most vulnerable within society who are at risk.

Notes

1 References have not been included to avoid identifying the local authority.
2 The bibliographic details of this report have been left out to help maintain confidentiality of the research participants.

8

Public Education Unbounded

In writing this book I wanted to open up the conversation on where we might in future take public education. This would not be another dour account of the erosion of the public sector, although I recognize the extensive challenges to publicness in the modernization of education systems since the 1980s. Instead the book focuses on small instances of publicness to show that while education has been reshaped by neoliberal discourses that are promulgated through national and market governance, there are numerous resistances even within the locations where we might least expect to find them. While the victories for publicness within the educational contexts described throughout the book are small, the broader significance of the work is in its reconceptualization of public education. Public education needs an update based on contemporary understandings of publics and the individuals of which they are comprised. While I make no claim to having found the answer for what a contemporary public education should look like, reflection on the themes of this book led me to three principles from its theoretical framing that ought to underpin future discussion and recomposition of public education.

The first principle in opening up conversation on public education is to conceive of a pluralist notion of public education. The way we commonly define public education in terms of a unified and essential public is exclusionary and opposes democratic values of participation and equality. What democracy needs is a pluralist public education that is built on presumptions of difference and equality between different subjectivities. We need not be afraid of individualism if we remember that democracy in education is built upon a presupposition of collectivist individualism.

The second principle is based in the recognition that hard boundaries between different publics also lead to exclusion. Unbounded publics are legitimately free to self-govern and participate in the decisions that structure and give meaning to their lives; yet the presupposition of pluralist publics, emergence of publics around the exercise of self-rule and public opinion formed by multiple subjectivities means contestation and compromise are natural companions of democratic decision-making. Not all interests and needs can be met through the governance of actually existing publics; publicness is partial, and publics are conditional. Critical theory shows us that struggles between public and private interests in the educational contexts illustrated in earlier chapters are the struggles implicit in the realpolitik of public education. This is reassuring to a point, since it challenges the idea that privatization represents an inevitable decline in public education and reframes it as an expression of the ongoing struggle between the interests of individuals over collective good. Yet it is hard to find comfort when significant compromises are made to conditions of well-being, and life opportunities are curtailed.

Therefore, a third principle for future public education is to pay attention to the strength and quality of relations within unbounded, pluralist publics. When judging the quality of a pluralist public we need to examine the strength and quality of public opinion (is it formed from experience and engagement with systematized knowledge?) and relations between participating individuals (are they mutual or competitive?). While the examples of publicness illustrated in the book were in most cases notably weak in strength and quality, looking at them as characteristics of public rather than private spheres highlights what within them is not public and therefore what needs to be worked upon. It requires effort to see the co-operative local authority in Chapter 7 not as an exercise in privatization of local government services and dissolution of its democratic mandate but as a struggle to retain democracy, especially considering the reported difficulties in enacting democratic values. Small instances of publicness can compound, and so the efforts of LA4 might also be seen and strengthened within combined or joined-up co-operative local authority activity such as the cities of service initiatives within the Co-operative Councils' Innovation Network, a network of twenty-six local authorities (Hadfield, 2019). The examination of the pluralistic, conditional and unbounded publicness of local authorities is an area that deserves closer examination, especially as it has developed in England while central government has been distracted by Brexit negotiations and preparation.

As a concluding statement the principles I have outlined in this section are examined in the policy-in-use context of legislation for state-funded, autonomous schooling: first, outlining the restrictions on publicness experienced by three schools in Cornwall that sought to exercise democratic governance through their recontextualization of the self-managing academies programme; second, extending a proposal for New Zealand's reform of self-governing Tomorrow's

Schools by examining it in light of my proposed principles for future discussion on public education.

Recontextualization in the academies programme

In 2008 three secondary schools sent to the Department of Children, Families and Schools an expression of interest to join as a consortium the academies programme (identified by the pseudonyms Worthfield, Dale and Wickbury in a research study). At that time the academies programme was in its first phase, a school improvement initiative that set out to overturn entrenched cycles of deprivation within particular communities and '"turn around" underachieving schools' in the secondary sector (Curtis et al., 2008, p. 75). The origins of the academies programme lay with the New Labour government and its City Academies, which were intended to draw upon the expertise of sponsors to support urban schools in areas of high disadvantage to raise low attainment (Glatter, 2012; Gunter and McGinity, 2014). The sponsors of the first three City Academies reflected some of the different kinds of interests that have since become commonplace in the governance of state-funded schooling, reported in the media to include a philanthropist and chair of several large companies, a 'not-for-profit' educational services and consultancy organization, the Church of England and multinational telecommunications companies (BBC, 2000). By September 2001 the first three sponsored City Academies were ready to open, and these first tentative steps can now be seen as critical developments in an ongoing policy trend towards 'school autonomy' (Glatter, 2012). Relationships between City Academies and their sponsors and their relative freedom from local authority oversight were departures from mainstream schooling policy.

The schools were located in Cornwall, a county with a strong regional identity and, located on a peninsula in the far south-west, relatively geographically isolated from other parts of England. The physical location of Cornwall presents challenges for economic and social development, and its marginality is reflected in government statistics that identify Cornwall as a region of considerable social deprivation (Government Office for the South West, 2006). The schools were in discussions for sponsorship with the University of Plymouth and Cornwall College, and Cornwall Local Authority also played a prominent role. Through their consortium they aimed to 'transform the prospects for young people ... by raising to new peaks their levels of achievement and of other outcomes, including crucially, participation in Higher Education' (Strategy document, n.d., ¶1).

I worked with a team of researchers from the University of Plymouth to examine how different constituencies within the school communities of Worthfield and Dale were framing aspirations for their students. Responses suggested the regional location of the schools was generally perceived to be a disadvantage, with evidence of stereotypical expectations that high-achieving students would move out of the region for higher education initially and later on work, leaving behind lower achieving students who were less likely to move from school to higher education. While their proposed change to a consortium of academy schools was a deliberate attempt to turn around these negative perceptions, this was not to be the case because the academies proposal was turned down by the Department of Children, Families and Schools.

By May 2010 the government had changed to a Conservative Liberal-Democrat coalition, and not long afterwards the academies programme was vastly expanded by rushing through the Academies Act 2010. In 2008, towards the end of the Labour government's time in power, there were 130 schools in the academies programme, by 2016 there were 5,549 academies.[1] Curtis et al. (2008) identified three original ultimate objectives of the academies programme, including: (1) raising achievement by 'breaking the cycle of underachievement and low aspirations in areas of deprivation with historical low performance' (p. 5); (2) increasing school diversity and choice; and (3) creating inclusive and mixed ability schools. The Academies Act 2010 overrode the first objective by offering conversion by choice to schools deemed successful because they were rated as good or above by Ofsted, the inspectorate for state-funded schools. It also made changes to the relationship between academies and external sponsors, allowing successful schools to develop their own academy trusts and act as standalone academies, or in some cases to become sponsors for other schools perceived to be less successful. While many schools chose not to convert to academies, especially primary schools, some schools that were deemed to be unsuccessful found themselves compelled to convert and adopt a sponsor. During the course of the study Dale and Wickbury reapplied for academy status under the changed criteria, although separately, and Wickbury was granted an order that enabled it to make the transition to an academy school. Like many secondary academy converters, the schools were opting for a school structure that promised them greater autonomy over curriculum and resourcing issues. There is promise in autonomous schooling for communities where locality is an obvious contributing factor to student success in school and the life opportunities associated with schooling. The potential of autonomy, albeit not actually facilitated by the academies programme, is that local communities can act on issues of significance to their localities and address local needs.

What I originally saw in the private Sands School was a small, localized public that came together to form opinions and make decisions on issues that affected its constituent members. Closer analysis revealed the regulation of some school practices coming from discourses of the state, market and the interimbrication of both state and market. While these interpolations represented a compromise to the school's democratic ideals, the philosophy of democracy remained significantly influential in school practices. The extent and depth of democracy was not ideal but still substantial. This is a conditional counterpublic sphere, in which self-governing yet reciprocally constitutive individuals have created a jurisdiction (the school) where they exercise accountability to one another. The conditions upon the school's counterpublicness come from accountability to the state and accountability to education consumers. The counterpublic deliberates on and develops its own internal charters, but it must still conform to the financial regulation of company law, submit evidence of public benefit to the Charity Commission and respect the rules of assessment set out by England's qualifications regulator Ofqual. An influence that is even further dislocated from democracy is the pernicious influence on the counterpublic of market relations. While the public of Sands sought its own jurisdiction in the private schooling sector, where it is further removed from the influence of state education policy than most schools that are in the state school sector, this location brings with it a closer relationship to the educational marketplace. This relationship restricts its capacity to be a public. The charging of school fees restricts the freedom of individuals to attend the school, and thus association with the schools' related counterpublic, but it also has implications for collective rights through its restrictions on freedom to associate. As a fee-charging school it is restricted from associating with other democratic publics, it is very distant from local government and set apart from its geographically local community. It is its desire for self-sufficiency in respect of governance that makes it less democratic.

More closely aligned with the academies programme is Discovery 1 School discussed at the beginning of the book. Discovery 1 also sought its own jurisdiction, but as a free, state school with its own special character rather than as a fee-charging school. While it was closer to the mainstream public and therefore national democratic governance through the state regulation of schooling, it was less successful in and perhaps less desiring of instituting democratic practices within the school. More significant influences evident throughout the early days of the school were bureaucracy and business practices. The challenges the school faced recur in many examples of schools that seek sovereignty through policies of school autonomy, such as the academies programme. Like Yeatman's (2007) concept of the ideal sovereign individual, who is apparently self-sufficient yet is integrally dependent upon the collective, autonomous schools are illusory (Boyask, 2018). They appear to have control of resource decisions but are actually hooked into relations of dependency and control, and decisions are not made through democratic deliberation and decision-making but through 'tactical interpretation rather than actual strategizing' (Higham and Earley, 2013, p. 704). While the academies programme promises schools like Worthfield, Dale and Wickbury the power to redefine their own destinies according to local need, they may only exercise what Simkins (1997) calls operational rather than criteria or defining power. The failure of autonomous school policies like charter schools, free schools and academies to support the development of schools governed by democratic publics is an important background element in the story of this book, but not its focus. What is of greater interest is the continual re-emergence of the desire for participatory governance. Schools like Worthfield, Dale and Wickbury want to respond better to the interests of their communities. As academies they would be public education institutions in its broadest sense, but the concept of public in the academies version of public education is lacking in clarity of definition and purpose.

Policy to support democratic publics

The Cornish schools have some circumstances common to all other schools, some circumstances they share with subgroups of schools and some circumstances that are unique. Public education needs to accommodate the diversity of interests represented within this scenario. Refining the notion of public in public education to pluralist publics provides a firmer ground from which to construct an inclusive and participatory education system. A pluralist conceptualization of the public sphere opens governance to decisions informed by a wider group of opinions, based on the experiences of a wider group of people. However, pluralism on its own does not mean decisions taken will be informed by an informed public opinion or be taken by those who hold legitimate interests in the group. As discussed in Chapter 2 public opinion is limited by the quality of experiences had by the public. In the early twentieth century Lippman and Dewey were debating the limits of public opinion. Common schooling failed to educate broadly enough to govern all specialisms within a complex and differentiated society. While mass media spread broad and new knowledge as if circulated throughout a public sphere, both Lippman and Dewey agreed that opinion formed by news did not constitute the kind of deep knowledge needed for deliberative decision-making. In the present day new media broadcasts ideas from an ever-wider group of people. Yet Facebook and Twitter are perfect examples of how a platform that permits a diversity of views to be put forward does not represent democratic participation. Social media arguably do not constitute public spheres because even though circulation of discourse to a wide audience occurs, there are hidden restrictions on debate and opinion formation (Fuchs, 2013; Azumah, 2015). The restrictions include restrictions of access for individuals to material and cultural resources, and restrictions to freedom of association because powerful organizations or voices monopolize public discourse and crowd out critics. Yet, there are grounds for conceiving social media as an environment for pluralist and emergent publics. From a culturalist perspective Warner (2002) argues that there are seven premises underpinning the modern conception of a public: (1) A public is self-organized; (2) a public is a relation among strangers; (3) the address of public speech is both personal and impersonal; (4) a public is constituted through mere attention; (5) a public is the social space created by the reflexive circulation of discourse; (6) publics act historically according to the temporality of their circulation; (7) a public is poetic world-making. This definition is typical of an emergence-orientated perspective on the nature of the public that Mahony and Stephansen (2017) define thus:

> Emergence-oriented accounts emphasize the mediated, reflexive and indeterminate qualities of publics, proceeding from the assumption that the public is 'not best thought of as a pre-existing collective subject that straightforwardly expresses itself or offers itself up to be represented' (Mahony et al., 2010: 2). Rather, the interest is in how publics can be understood in the plural (Calhoun, 1997), how they may be called into existence through different modes of address and nurtured by different types of material or technological support (Jackson, 2011; Marres, 2012) and how these processes of mediation can be shaped by the agency and self-organization of multiple social subjects variously affected by issues at hand. (Warner, 2002, p. 40)

This is one of three general ways of conceptualizing publics that Mahony and Stephansen identified through their examination of recent academic literature and included in their public-centric conceptual framework. Another is conceiving of a public as a concrete entity that is knowable through calculative techniques, such as surveys and polls. This view of publics I associate with the notion of boundary from political philosophy. The public as a defined and knowable group is dependent upon some form of pre-legitimizing criteria to create its boundaries, such as in the case of a democratic nation state where the criteria for legitimacy comes through commonality in culture or ethnicity prior to a state of democracy. Yet pre-legitimacy delegitimizes the democratic character of a public, because the legitimacy of democracy is served 'not by tradition, not by virtue, not by genealogy, but by the demos itself' (Abizadeh, 2012). A fundamental principle of democratic self-rule is that the exercise of political power upon the people is in accordance with the laws determined by the people.

Mahony and Stephansen's (2017) third conceptualization of a public is a normative public. This is a public defined through philosophy or ideal, especially through the ideal of democracy. They highlight the influence of Habermas in this field, as well as

> work that has highlighted the exclusionary tendencies of the Habermasian model of the public sphere and the democratic importance of 'counter-publics' (Negt and Kluge, 1993; Fraser, 1990), work that has proposed a model of democracy based on 'agonistic pluralism' (Mouffe, 2002; Dahlberg, 2007), and work that has pointed to the Eurocentric history and underpinnings of the concept of the public sphere (Sousa Santos, 2012). (p. 39)

Yet, Mahony and Stephansen argue this view of publics is inconsistent with an emergence theory of publics, because publics are defined through a normative theory of democracy rather than through the public's practices of engagement. In effect this suggests that a boundary is established through a shared culture of democracy. A tentative and partial resolution lies in the conceptualization of democracy as practice and moving to the position that the legitimacy of the people is not predefined by a democratic ideal but emerges from the practice of self-rule by all who are subjected to the rule (Fraser, 2010; Abizadeh, 2012). This is a concept of an unbounded public, because the 'who' of the public is established through its constitution as a collective engaged in the work of self-governance.

An emergence orientation to public education without democracy weakens its publicness. A non-democratically constituted public is constituted through exercise of control external to the public. The power relations that bring it into being may be hidden, and some individuals affected by its power are excluded from decision-making. Autonomous schools are a case in point, where schools have emerged in response to governing policies that only apparently give control to schools and other affected members of the community. Schools in England engaging with the academies programme find themselves drastically restricted in the extent of their decision-making, whether that's the decision to convert, choosing sponsors or implicit or explicit coercion into joining a multi-academy trust. There is also broader influence on the immediate school community. Local authorities find themselves compelled to take decisions as a result of loss of funding through academization. Examples throughout this book have shown a commitment of many different kinds of entity to principles of equality and inclusive participation in decision-making, even when the extent of decision-making is compromised. Acceptance of the partial and conditional nature of publicness is also important for the future of public education. Once the aspects of education that have been privatized are opened up to public scrutiny, decisions can be made about the quality of compromise required. Public scrutiny however requires an informed public to scrutinize. Dewey highlighted the important role of education in deepening public opinion and clarifying the role of the public in respect of decision-making. The role of publics is to deliberate and select those best placed to work in its interests within the different facets of a complex society. Therefore, what we want from public education policy is not a set of regulations handed to us by the politicians elected, but a set of education policies that have been constructed by education specialists who are working in consultation with and on behalf of the people. What this might look like is hinted at by a recent proposal for education reform in New Zealand, albeit not through the proposal itself nor by the policy that ultimately developed, but by what the proposal might have been.

Tomorrow's Schools (1989) was an initiative of New Zealand's fourth Labour government that was proposed by non-educationalists and set about reforming school administration and governance by making them autonomous units overseen by individual board of trustees. This is how all state-funded New Zealand schools have continued to operate since then. However, a recent government-appointed taskforce (Tomorrow's Schools Independent Taskforce, 2018) recommended a reorganization of governance, so that the powers of boards are restricted to school vision and teaching and learning, and the governing of resource allocation would be redeployed to middle-tier education hubs. This is in a country where local government has no responsibility at all for education, and even regional ministry of education offices are small with limited responsibilities. The proposed hubs were to be crown agencies, independent of the state, yet accountable to it, and governed by ministerial-appointed directors. While the aim of the proposed change was to reduce the inequities in the quality of governance brought about through the segregating effects of an autonomous school system, New Zealand's education hubs limited in different kinds of way participation in decision-making.

The principles outlined at the beginning of this chapter and identified as important to progressing conversations of public can be applied to this policy scenario. There is an element of pluralism implicit in this model, with the recognition that different needs and interests require a multi-faceted governance structure that includes national, regional and school-based governing bodies with different roles. The extent to which different voices might organize in different kinds of structures is unclear, and the model risks excluding some interests from participation in governance if the model becomes standardized. An example in New Zealand is indigenous Māori populations who, when operating in Te Ao Māori (or the Māori world), structure their lives in reference to their own ontologies and epistemologies. Ongoing scrutiny and revision of the structures may help the responsiveness to and inclusion of diverse subjectivities.

In current policy the board of trustees is a Crown entity responsible for governance of a school, brought together to govern the interests represented within the school. While the Crown evidently represents a bounded public, legitimized at a national level by citizenship and residency laws, the board of trustees model also has elements of boundedness because even though trustees are elected by 'the parent community, staff members and, in the case of schools with students above Year 9, the students' (Education Counts, 2019), that is convened through self-rule, most of the schools have admissions policies established on the basis of school zones or catchment areas. For parents and students, admission is a pre-legitimating criterion. The proposed regional hubs policy for a middle tier is also based upon locality.

The decision within the proposal to make the directors of their education hubs ministerial appointments rather than democratically elected public servants was an interesting one. It lengthens the distance of publics from decision-making. Yet, it also seems to be a response to the modern-day problem of the public, that is, public opinion is conflictual, based in a belief in self-sufficient individualism and informed by popular rather than systematized knowledge. The problem of properly preparing publics to take on public roles in democratic decision-making is vast, but recognition of the inevitability of compromise in less than ideal conditions for democracy means that the possibilities for public participation do not end there. It could start within regional education hubs through putting the decision of who to elect to the public, with some limits. For example, establishing a set of criteria for nominations to posts within the educational hubs based upon expertise in education. It would move us away from a model of governance, where important decisions that affect schools are made by distant politicians, and governing experts, a class set apart from the common interests of the public for whom they are appointed.

Closing thoughts

Some of the educational settings that have been examined are closer to democratic public education than others, and these may be understood as conditional counterpublics. However, all the educational settings examined exhibit some properties of publicness. These partial and conditional forms of public education work as sites in which we can test out, challenge and revise the normative construction of public education.

By recognizing, conceptualizing and reappraising the public characteristics of educational sites even when they fall short of those of an ideal democratic public sphere this book has gone beyond critique of contemporary public education. Making apparent and clarifying the public dimensions of weakened public education can help to strengthen these dimensions as the ideal takes hold of the social imagination. The book has also argued that private interests in education should not automatically be a criterion for exclusion from what is considered public education, because at times private institutions keep democratic equality within sight when it is marginalized elsewhere; for example, when strong albeit conditional counterpublics that draw upon democratic and participatory philosophies are formed within the private school sector. Furthermore, taking a social perspective means recognizing that private involvement in public education is essentially social, like all other forms of human endeavour, and that clear distinctions between public and private education only serve to exclude private involvement from public scrutiny and deliberation. Making the private public should provide opportunities for debate, deliberation, opinion formation and decision-making about new conceptualizations of public education.

References

Abizadeh, A. (2012). 'On the Demos and Its Kin: Nationalism, Democracy, and the Boundary Problem'. *American Political Science Review*, 106(4): 867–82.

Abowitz, K. K. (2010). 'Qualifying My Faith in the Common School Ideal: A Normative Framework for Democratic Justice'. *Educational Theory*, 60(6): 683–702. https://doi.org/doi:10.1111/j.1741-5446.2010.00384.x.

Aghion, P., Besley, T., Browne, J., Caselli, F., Lambert, R., Lomax, R., Pissarides, C., Stern, N. and Van Reenee, J. (2013). *Investing for Prosperity: Skills, Infrastructure and Innovation, Report of the LSE Growth Commission*. London: LSE.

Altbach, P. G., and Knight, J. (2007). 'The Internationalization of Higher Education: Motivations and Realities'. *Journal of Studies in International Education*, 11(3–4): 290–305. doi:10.1177/1028315307303542.

Anderson, G. (2017). 'Privatizing Subjectivities: How New Public Management (NPM) Is Designing a "New" Professional in Education'. *Revista Brasileira de Política e Administração da Educação*, 33(3): 561–92.

Arnot, M. (2002). 'The Complex Gendering of Invisible Pedagogies: Social Reproduction or Empowerment?' *British Journal of Sociology of Education*, 23(4): 583–93.

Atkinson, P. (1985). *Language Structure and Reproduction: An Introduction to the Sociology of Basil Bernstein*. London: Methuen.

Azumah, D. C. (2015). 'Blogging as Public Pedagogy: Creating Alternative Educational Futures'. *International Journal of Lifelong Education*, 34(3): 284–99.

Ball, S. (1993). 'What Is Policy? Texts, Trajectories and Toolboxes'. *Discourse: Studies in the Cultural Politics of Education*, 13(2): 10–17. doi:10.1080/0159630930130203.

Ball, S. (2006). *Education Policy and Social Class: The Selected Works of Stephen J. Ball*. London: Routledge.

Ball, S. J. (2009). 'Privatising Education, Privatising Education Policy, Privatising Educational Research: Network Governance and the "Competition State"'. *Journal of Education Policy*, 24(1): 83–99. https://doi.org/10.1080/02680930802419474.

Ball, S., and Exley, S. (2010). 'Making Policy with "Good Ideas": Policy Networks and the "Intellectuals" of New Labour'. *Journal of Education Policy*, 25(2): 151–69.

Ball, S. J., and Bowe, R. (1992). 'Subject Departments and the "Implementation" of National Curriculum Policy: An Overview of the Issues'. *Journal of Curriculum Studies*, 24(2): 97–115. doi:10.1080/0022027920240201.

Ball, S. J., and Youdell, D. (2008). 'Hidden Privatisation in Public Education'. Retrieved from Brussels: http://pages.ei-ie.org/quadrennialreport/2008/upload/content_trsl_images/867/Hidden_privatisation_study-EN.pdf (accessed 18 March 2019).

BBC (2000). 'City Academies' to Tackle School Failure'. Retrieved 17 March 2016. http://news.bbc.co.uk/1/hi/education/925378.stm (accessed 17 March 2016).

BBC (2014). 'Ofsted Could Inspect Private Schools, Says Gove'. http://www.bbc.co.uk/news/education-27341805 (accessed 15 October 2015).

Beck, U. (1996). 'World Risk Society as Cosmopolitan Society?: Ecological Questions in a Framework of Manufactured Uncertainties'. *Theory, Culture & Society*, 13(4): 1–32. doi:10.1177/0263276496013004001.

Beck, U. and Beck-Gernsheim, E. (2002). 'Individualization: Institutionalized Individualism and Its Social and Political Consequences'. London: SAGE.

Benn, M., and Downs, J. (2015). *The Truth about Our Schools: Exposing the Myths, Exploring the Evidence*. London: Routledge.

Bernstein, B. ([1971] 1973). *Class, Codes and Control: Volume I: Theoretical Studies towards a Sociology of Language*, St Albans: Paladin.

Bernstein, B. (2000). *Pedagogy, Symbolic Control, and Identity*. Blue Ridge Summit: Rowman & Littlefield.

Bernstein, B. (2001). 'Symbolic Control: Issues of Empirical Description of Agencies and Agents'. *International Journal of Social Research Methodology*, 4(1): 21–33.

Bernstein, B. ([1975] 2003). *Class, Codes and Control: Volume III: Towards a Theory of Educational Transmission*. London: Routledge.

Bevir, M. (2012). *Governance: A Very Short Introduction*. Oxford: Oxford University Press.

Biesta, G., and Burbules, N. C. (2003). *Pragmatism and Educational Research*: Lanham, MD: Rowman & Littlefield.

Biesta, G. (2016). 'Education and Democracy Revisited: Dewey's Democratic Deficit'. In S. Higgins and F. Coffield (eds), *John Dewey's Democracy and Education : A British Tribute*. London: UCL Institute of Education Press, pp. 149–69. Retrieved from http://ebookcentral.proquest.com/lib/aut/detail.action?docID=5302067.

Blackmore, J. (2016). *Educational Leadership and Nancy Fraser*. London: Routledge.

Boostrom, R. (2016). 'The Peculiar Status of Democracy and Education'. *Journal of Curriculum Studies*, 48(1): 4–22. doi:10.1080/00220272.2014.962100.

Bourdieu, P., and Passeron, J.-C. (1990). *Reproduction in Education, Society and Culture*, 2nd edn. London: Sage.

Boyask, R. (2012). 'Advancing Relations between Qualitative Methodology and Social Theory in the Sociology of Education'. In S. Delamont (ed.), *Handbook of Qualitative Research in Education*. Cheltenham: Elgar, pp. 21–31.

Boyask, R. (2013). 'Theorising the Democratic Potential of Privatised Schools through the Case of Free Schools'. *ACCESS: Critical Perspectives on Communication, Cultural and Policy Studies*, 32(1/2): 11–26.

Boyask, R. (2015a). 'Nuanced Understandings of Privatization in Local Authorities' Services to Schools'. *Management in Education*, 29(1): 35–40.

Boyask, R. (2015b). *Social Justice in Privatised Schooling* (Report prepared for British Academy, 2013). Retrieved from http://www.ruthboyask.com/social_justice_in_ privatised_schooling (accessed 9 January 2015).

Boyask, R. (2015c). 'The Public Good in English Private School Governance'. *European Educational Research Journal*, 14(6): 566–81.

Boyask, R. (2018). 'Primary School Autonomy in the Context of the Expanding Academies Programme'. *Educational Management Administration and Leadership*, 46(1): 107–23.

Boyask, R., McPhail, J. C., Kaur, B. and O'Connell, K. (2008). 'Democracy at Work in and through Experimental Schooling'. *Discourse: Studies in the Cultural Politics of Education*, 29(1): 19–34. doi:10.1080/01596300701801286.

Brewer, D., and Hentschke, G. (2009). 'An International Perspective on Publicly-Financed, Privately-Operated Schools'. In M. Berends, M. G. Springer, D. Ballou and H. J. Walberg (eds), *Handbook of Research on School Choice*. New York: Routledge, pp. 227–46.

Brown, P. (1990). 'The Third Wave: Education and the Ideology of Parentocracy'. *British Journal of Sociology of Education*, 11(1): 65–85.

Burawoy, M. (1998). 'The Extended Case Method'. *Sociological Theory*, 16(1): 4–33.

Carnie, F. (2003). *Alternative Approaches to Education: A Guide for Parents and Teachers*. London: Routledge.

Chaddad, F. (2012). 'Advancing the Theory of the Cooperative Organization: The Cooperative as True Hybrid'. *Annals of Public and Cooperative Economics*, (83)4: 445–61.

Charities Services (n.d.). 'Public Benefit and Charitable Purpose'. Retrieved from https://www.charities.govt.nz/apply-for-registration/charitable-purpose/public-benefit-and-charitable-purpose/ (accessed 31 August 2018).

Charity Commission (2013). What Makes a Charity?, Retrieved 12 December 2014, https://www.gov.uk/government/publications/what-makes-a-charity-cc4/what-makes-a-charity-cc4#part-4-about-the-public-benefit-requirement.

Chell, E. (2007). 'Social Enterprise and Entrepreneurship: Towards a Convergent Theory of the Entrepreneurial Process'. *International Small Business Journal*, 25(1), 5–26. doi:10.1177/0266242607071779.

Coates, M. (2015). 'The Co-operative: Good with Schools?' *Management in Education*, 29(1): 14–19. doi:10.1177/0892020614560839.

Cohen, M. (2004). 'Gender and the Private/ Public Debate on Education in the Long Eighteenth Century'. In R. Aldrich (ed.), *Public or Private Education? Lessons from History*. Routledge. Retrieved from https://ebookcentral.proquest.com/lib/aut/detail. action?docID=183078.

Courtney, S. J. (2015). 'Mapping School Types in England'. *Oxford Review of Education*, 41(6), 799–818. doi:10.1080/03054985.2015.1121141.

Curtis A., Exley, S., Sasia, A., Tough, S. and Whitty, G. (2008) *The Academies Programme: Progress, Problems and Possibilities*. London: The Sutton Trust.

Curtis, T. (2008). 'Finding that grit makes a pearl: A critical re-reading of research into social enterprise'. *International Journal of Entrepreneurial Behaviour & Research*, 14(5): 276–90.

Davies B., and Bansel, P. (2007) 'Neoliberalism and Education'. *International Journal of Qualitative Studies in Education*, 20(3): 247–59.

Davies, B., and Hentschke, G. (2006). 'Public–Private Partnerships in Education: Insights from the Field'. *School Leadership & Management*, 26(3): 205–26. doi:10.1080/13632430600736977.

Davies, I., and Chong, E. K. M. (2016). 'Current Challenges for Citizenship Education in England'. *Asian Education and Development Studies*, 5(1): 20–36. doi:10.1108/AEDS-05-2015-0015.

Dennis, J. (2017). 'Imagining Powerful Co-Operative Schools: Theorising Dynamic Co-Operation with Spinoza'. *Educational Philosophy and Theory*, 1–9. doi:10.1080/00131857.2017.1382350.

Department for Business, Energy & Industrial Strategy (DfBEIS) (2016). *Office of the Regulator of Community Interest Companies: Information and Guidance Notes*. Cardiff: DBEIS.

Department for Education (DfE) (2010a). Michael Gove Invites all Schools to Become Academies. In the News. Retrieved from http://www.education.gov.uk/inthenews/inthenews/a0061072/michael-gove-invites-all-schools-to-become-academies (accessed 18 October 2010).

Department for Education (DfE) (2010b). *The Importance of Teaching: The Schools White Paper 2010*. London: The Stationery Office.

Department for Education (DfE) (2014). *Opening a Free School*, Retrieved from https://www.gov.uk/government/collections/opening-a-free-school (accessed 11 April 2014).

Department for Education (DfE) (2019a). *The Independent School Standards: Guidance for Independent Schools*. London: Department for Education.

Department for Education (DfE) (2019b). *The Proportion of Pupils in Academies and Free Schools, in England, in October 2018: Ad-hoc Notice: January 2019*. London: Department for Education.

Department for Education and Employment (DfEE) (2001). *Schools: Building on Success – Raising Standards, Promoting Diversity, Achieving Results*. Norwich: The Stationary Office.

Dewey, J. ([1899] 1915). *The School and Society*. Chicago: University of Chicago Press.

Dewey, J. (1916). *Democracy and Education: An Introduction to the Philosophy of Education*. New York: Macmillan.

Dewey, J. ([1927] 2016). *The Public and Its Problems: An Essay in Political Inquiry*, Ohio University Press. ProQuest Ebook Central, http://ebookcentral.proquest.com/lib/aut/detail.action?docID=4722628.

Di Maggio, P. J., and Powell, W. (1983). 'The Iron Cage Revisited: Institutional Isomorphism and Collective Rationality in Organizational Fields'. *American Sociological Review*, 48(2): 147–60.

Durkheim, E. ([1893] 1984). *The Division of Labour in Society*. London: Macmillan.

Dymond, S., Chun, E., Kim, R. and Renzaglia, A. (2013). 'A Validation of Elements, Methods, and Barriers to Inclusive High School Service-Learning Programs'. *Remedial and Special Education*, 34(5): 293–304.

Education Counts (2019). Boards of Trustees. Retrieved from https://www.educationcounts.govt.nz/data-services/data collections/national/boards_of_trustees (accessed 27 July 2019).

Education Review Office (2006). *Confirmed Education Review Report: Discovery 1 School*. Christchurch: Education Review Office: Canterbury Office.

External Reporting Board (2015). *New Zealand Accounting Standards Framework*. Retrieved from https://www.xrb.govt.nz/dmsdocument/2541 (accessed 28 June 2016).

Fairburn, C. (2013). *Charitable Status and Independent Schools*. London: House of Commons Library.

Feinberg, W. (2012). 'The Idea of a Public Education'. *Review of Research in Education*, 36(1): 1–22. doi:10.3102/0091732X11421114.

Feinstein, N. W. (2015). 'Education, Communication, and Science in the Public Sphere'. *Journal of Research in Science Teaching*, 52(2): 145–63. doi:10.1002/tea.21192.

Fielding, M., and Moss, P. (2010). *Radical Education and the Common School: A Democratic Alternative*. London: Routledge.

Fraser, N. (1990). 'Rethinking the Public Sphere: A Contribution to the Critique of Actually Existing Democracy'. *Social Text* (25/26): 56–80. doi:10.2307/466240.

Fraser, N. (2008). 'Abnormal Justice'. *Critical Inquiry*, 34(3): 393–422. doi:10.1086/589478.

Fraser, N. (2010). *Scales of Justice: Reimagining Political Space in a Globalizing World*. New York: Columbia University Press, 2010. Pbk. edition.

Fraser, N. (2014). 'Transnationalizing the Public Sphere: On the Legitimacy and Efficacy of Public Opinion in a Post-Westphalian World'. In K. Nash (ed.), *Transnationalizing the Public Sphere*. Cambridge: Polity Press, pp. 8–42.

Fuchs, C. (2013). *Social Media: A Critical Introduction*. London: SAGE.

Gerrard, J. (2015). 'Public Education in Neoliberal Times: Memory and Desire'. *Journal of Education Policy*, 30(6): 855–68. doi:10.1080/02680939.2015.1044568.

Gerrard, J., Savage, G. C. and O'Connor, K. (2017). 'Searching for the Public: School Funding and Shifting Meanings of "the Public" in Australian Education'. *Journal of Education Policy*, 32(4): 503–19. doi:10.1080/02680939.2016.1274787.

Gewirtz, S., Ball, S. and Bowe, R. (1995). *Markets, Choice, and Equity in Education*. Buckingham: Open University Press.

Giles, C. (2014). 'IMF Warns on Threat of Income Inequality'. *Financial Times*, 19 January 2014. Retrieved from http://www.ft.com/cms/s/0/b3462520-805b-11e3-853f-00144feab7de.html (accessed 25 March 2014).

Glatter, R. (2012). 'Persistent Preoccupations: The Rise and Rise of School Autonomy and Accountability in England'. *Educational Management Administration & Leadership*, 40(5): 559–75.

Glatter, R. (2017). '"Because We Can": Pluralism and Structural Reform in Education'. *London Review of Education*, 15(1): 115–25.

Glover, S. I., Fontenot, L. A., and Korn, H. A. (2016). 'A Corporate Paradigm Shift: Public Benefit Corporations'. *Insights*, 30(10): 17–22.

Gomm, R., Hammersley, M. and Foster, P. (2002). 'Case Study and Generalization'. In R. Gomm, M. Hammersley and P. Foster (eds), *Case Study Method: Key Issues, Key Texts*. London: Sage.

Gorard, S. (2014). 'The Link between Academies in England, Pupil Outcomes and Local Patterns of Socio-Economic Segregation between Schools'. *Research Papers in Education*, 29(3): 268–84. doi:10.1080/02671522.2014.885726.

Gordon, M. (2016). 'Why Should Scholars Keep Coming Back to John Dewey?' *Educational Philosophy and Theory*, 48(10): 1077–91. doi:10.1080/00131857.2016.1150800.

Gordon, M., and English, A. R. (2016). 'John Dewey's Democracy and Education in an Era of Globalization'. *Educational Philosophy and Theory*, 48(10): 977–80. doi:10.1080/00131857.2016.1204742.

Gove, M. (2012, 5 July). Michael Gove on FASNA's first twenty years: Speech. Retrieved from https://www.gov.uk/government/speeches/michael-gove-on-fasnas-first-twenty-years (accessed 14 August 2013).

Government Office for the South West (2006). *Poverty & Deprivation in Cornwall: An analysis at Census Output Area Level*. Government Office for the South West.

Gunter, H. M., Hall, D. and Mills, C. (2015). 'Consultants, Consultancy and Consultocracy in Education Policymaking in England'. *Journal of Education Policy*, 30(4): 518–39. doi:10.1080/02680939.2014.963163.

Gunter, H., and McGinity, R. (2014). 'The Politics of the Academies Programme: Natality and Pluralism in Education Policy-Making'. *Research Papers in Education*, 29(3): 300–14. doi:10.1080/02671522.2014.885730.

Gunter, H. M., and Mills, C. (2017). *Consultants and Consultancy: The Case of Education*. Cham, Switzerland: Springer.

Habermas, J. ([1962] 1991). *The Structural Transformation of the Public Sphere: An Inquiry into a Category of Bourgeoisie Society*. Cambridge, MA: MIT Press.

Hadfield, M. (2019). 'How Do We Build Co-Operative Places? CCIN Prepares for National Conference'. *Coop News*. Retrieved from https://www.thenews.coop/142295/topic/politics/how-do-we-build-co-operative-places-ccin-prepares-for-national-conference/ (accessed 20 January 2020).

Hammersley, M., Gomm, R. and Foster, P. (2002). 'Case Study and Theory'. In R. Gomm, M. Hammersley and P. Foster (eds), *Case Study Method: Key Issues, Key Texts*. London: Sage.

Hastings, A., Bailey, N., Bramley, G., Gannon, M. and Watkins, D. (2015). *The Cost of the Cuts: The Impact on Local Government and Poorer Communities* (J. R. Foundation Ed.). York.

Hatcher, R. (2014). 'Local Authorities and the School System: The New Authority-Wide Partnerships'. *Educational Management, Administration & Leadership*, 42(3): 355–71.

Heilbronn, R., Doddington, C. and Higham, R. (eds) (2018). *Dewey and Education in the 21st Century: Fighting Back*. Bingley: Emerald.

Higham, R., and Biddulph, J. (2018). 'How Has Dewey's Democratic Theory Influenced the Development of a New Primary School? A Headteacher's Perspective'. *Education 3–13*, 46(4): 385–92. doi:10.1080/03004279.2018.1445472.

Higham, R., and Earley, P. (2013). 'School Autonomy and Government Control: School Leaders' Views on a Changing Policy Landscape in England'. *Educational Management Administration & Leadership*, 41(6): 701–17.

Hodge, G. A., and Greve, C. (2007). 'Public–Private Partnerships: An International Performance Review'. *Public Administration Review*, 67(3): 545–58. doi:10.1111/j.1540-6210.2007.00736.x.

Hunt, T. (24 November 2014). 'Private Schools Have Done Too Little for Too Long'. *Guardian*, http://www.theguardian.com/commentisfree/2014/nov/24/private-schools-independent-sector-state-system (accessed 5 March 2015).

IDEN (2010). IDEN: What Is Democratic Education? http://www.idenetwork.org/what-is-democratic-education.htm (accessed 31 May 2011).

Independent Schools Council (ISC) (2013). *ISC Census 2013*. London: Independent Schools Council.

Independent Schools Council (ISC) (2018). *ISC Census and Annual Report 2018*. London: Independent Schools Council.

Karlsson, J. (2006). Affected and Subjected: The All-Affected Principle in Transnational Democratic Theory. Available at SSRN: https://ssrn.com/abstract=2274644 or http://dx.doi.org/10.2139/ssrn.2274644 (accessed 31 July 2018).

Keddie, A. (2018). 'Conceptions of Responsibility within and Beyond Neoliberal Frames'. *Educational Management Administration & Leadership*, 46(1): 124.

Kelly, C. (2014). *Failings in Management and Governance: Report of the Independent Review into the Events Leading to the Co-operative Bank's Capital Shortfall*, Retrieved fromhttp://www.thekellyreview.co.uk/final_report_2014.html (accessed 12 April 2017).

Khadaroo, I. (2014). 'The Valuation of Risk Transfer in UK School Public Private Partnership Contracts'. *The British Accounting Review*, 46(2): 154–65. doi:10.1016/j.bar.2013.12.004.

Knight Abowitz, K. (2001). 'Charter Schools and Social Justice'. *Educational Theory*, 51(2): 151–70.

Knight Abowitz, K. (2010). 'Qualifying My Faith in the Common School Ideal: A Normative Framework for Democratic Justice'. *Educational Theory*, 60(6): 683–702. doi:10.1111/j.1741-5446.2010.00384.x.

Knight Abowitz, K., and Karaba, R. (2010). 'Charter Schooling and Democratic Justice'. *Educational Policy*, 24: 534–58.

Koh, A., and Kenway, J. (2016). *Elite Schools: Multiple Geographies of Privilege*. New York: Routledge.

Koinzer, T., Nikolai, R. and Waldow, F. (2017). 'Private Schooling and School Choice as Global Phenomena: An Introduction'. In T. Koinzer, R. Nikolai and F. Waldow (eds), *Private Schools and School Choice in Compulsory Education: Global Change and National Challenge*. Wiesbaden: Springer Fachmedien Wiesbaden, pp. 1–6.

Kraftl, P. (2014). *Geographies of Alternative Education: Diverse Learning Spaces for Children and Young People*. Bristol: Policy Press.

Kurland, N. B. (2017). 'Accountability and the Public Benefit Corporation'. *Business Horizons*, 60(4): 519–28. doi:10.1016/j.bushor.2017.03.009.

Kynaston, D., and F. Green (2019). *Engines of Privilege: Britain's Private School Problem*. London: Bloomsbury.

Labaree, D. (1997). 'Public Goods, Private Goods: The American Struggle over Educational Goals'. *American Educational Research Journal*, 34(1): 39–81.

Labaree, D. (2007). *Education, Markets, and the Public Good: The Selected Works of David F. Labaree*. New York: Routledge.

Landow, P., and Ebdon, C. (2012). 'Public-Private Partnerships, Public Authorities, and Democratic Governance'. *Public Performance & Management Review*, 35(4): 727–52. doi:10.2753/PMR1530-9576350408.

Laureate Education (2015). Laureate Education Becomes a Public Benefit Corporation [Press release]. Retrieved from https://www.laureate.net/newsroom/pressreleases/2015/10/laureate-education-becomes-a-public-benefit-corporation (accessed 31 August 2018).

Laureate Education (2019). Laureate Education, Inc. – Investor Relations. Retrieved from http://investors.laureate.net/home/default.aspx.

Laureate International Universities (n.d.). Here for Good: The Laureate Code of Conduct and Ethics. Retrieved from https://www.laureate.net/wp-content/uploads/2019/04/Laureate_conduct_ethics_EN-1.pdf (accessed 22 July 2019).

Leat, D., and Reid, R. (2012). 'Exploring the Role of Student Researchers in the Process of Curriculum Development'. *Curriculum Journal*, 23(2): 189–205.

Levin, H. (1999). 'The Public–Private Nexus in Education'. *American Behavioral Scientist*, 43(1): 124. doi:10.1177/00027649921955191.

Levin, H. M., Cornelisz, I. and Hanisch-Cerda, B. (2013). 'Does Educational Privatisation Promote Social Justice? *Oxford Review of Education*, 39(4): 514–32. doi:10.1080/03054985.2013.825983.

Lingard, B., and Sellar, S. (2013). 'Globalization, Edu-Business and Network Governance: The Policy Sociology of Stephen J. Ball and rethinking Education Policy Analysis'. *London Review of Education*, 11(3): 265–80. doi:10.1080/14748460.2013.840986.

Lippmann, W. ([1922] 1997). *Public Opinion*. Somerset: Routledge.
Lubienski, C. (2001). 'Redefining "Public" Education: Charter Schools, Common Schools, and the Rhetoric of Reform'. *Teachers College Record*, 103(4): 634–66.
Lubienski, C. (2003). 'Innovation in Education Markets: Theory and Evidence on the Impact of Competition and Choice in Charter Schools'. *American Educational Research Journal*, 40(2): 395–443. http://aer.sagepub.com/content/40/2/395.
Lubienski, C. (2009). *Do Quasi-markets Foster Innovation in Education?: A Comparative Perspective*, OECD Education Working Papers, No. 25, OECD Publishing. http://dx.doi.org/10.1787/221583463325 (accessed 12 April 2017).
Lubienski, C., and Linick, M. (2011) 'Quasi-Markets and Innovation in Education'. *Die Deutsche Schule*, 103(2) (special issue on the economics of education): 139–57.
Low, C. (2006). 'A Framework for the Governance of Social Enterprise'. *International Journal of Social Economics*, 33(5/6): 376–85. doi:10.1108/03068290610660652.
Machin, S., and Vignoles, A. (2006). *Education Policy in the UK*. London: Centre for the Economics of Education.
Mahony, P., and Hextall, I. (2013). ' "Building Schools for the Future": "Transformation" for Social Justice or Expensive Blunder? *British Educational Research Journal*, 39(5): 853–871. doi:10.1002/berj.3001.
Mahony, P., Hextall, I. and Richardson, M. (2011). 'Building Schools for the Future': Reflections on a New Social Architecture'. *Journal of Education Policy*, 26(3): 341–60. doi:10.1080/02680939.2010.513741.
Mahony, N., and Stephansen, H. C. (2017). 'Engaging with the Public in Public Engagement with Research'. *Research for All*, 1(1): 35–51. doi:10.18546/rfa.01.1.04.
Mangez, E., and Hilgers, M. (2012). 'The Field of Knowledge and the Policy Field in Education: PISA and the Production of Knowledge for Policy'. *European Educational Research Journal*, 11(2): 189–205. doi:10.2304/eerj.2012.11.2.189.
Mann, H. (1957). *The Republic and the School: The Education of Free Men*. New York, US: Teachers College Press.
Mason, C., Kirkbride, J. and Bryde, D. (2007). 'From Stakeholders to Institutions: The Changing Face of Social Enterprise Governance Theory'. *Management Decision*, 45(2): 284–301. doi:10.1108/00251740710727296.
Mazzucato, M. (2013). *The Entrepreneurial State: Debunking Public vs. Private Sector Myths*. London: Anthem Press.
McPhail, J. C., and Palincsar, A. S. (2009). 'Discovery Meets Inquiry: A Cross-Cultural Essay', In K. Quinlivan, R. Boyask and B. Kaur (eds), *Educational Enactments in a Globalised World: Intercultural Conversations*. Rotterdam: Sense.
Millar, F. (2011). Private Schools Do Not Understand 'Public Benefit' http://www.theguardian.com/education/2011/may/10/private-schools-charitable-status (accessed 5 March 2015).
Mills, C. Wright. ([1959] 1970). *The Sociological Imagination*. Harmondsworth, Middlesex: Penguin Books.

Mills, M. (2015). 'The Tyranny of No Alternative: Co-Operating in a Competitive Marketplace'. *International Journal of Inclusive Education*, 19(11): 1172–89. doi:10.10 80/13603116.2015.1044204.

Mills, S. (2004). *Discourse*. London: Routledge, 2004.

Ministry of Housing, Communities, and Local Government (MHC&LG) (2018). Local Government Financial Statistics England. Retrieved from London: https://www.gov.uk/government/collections/local-government-finance-statistics-england (accessed 22 July 2017).

Miron, G., and Welner, K. G. (2012). 'Introduction'. In G. Miron, K. G. Welner, P. H. Hinchey and W. J. Mathis (eds), *Exploring the School Choice Universe: Evidence and Recommendations*. Charlotte: Information Age.

Morais, A. M. (2002). 'Basil Bernstein at the Micro Level of the Classroom'. *British Journal of Sociology of Education*, 23(4): 559–69. doi:10.1080/0142569022000038413.

Mundy, K., Green, A., Lingard, B. and Verger, A. (2016). *Handbook of Global Education Policy*. Somerset: John Wiley.

Naidoo, V. (2009). 'Transnational Higher Education: A Stock Take of Current Activity'. *Journal of Studies in International Education*, 13(3): 310–30. doi:10.1177/1028315308317938.

Nairn, K., and Smith, A. (2003) Young people as researchers in schools: The possibilities of peer research. Paper presented at *American Educational Research Association Conference*, Chicago, 21–25 April.

National Audit Office (2009). *The Building Schools for the Future Programme: Renewing the Secondary School Estate*. London: The Stationery Office.

Newman, J. (2007). 'Re-Mapping the Public: Public Libraries and the Public Sphere'. *Cultural Studies*, 21(6): 887–909.

Nixon, J. (2010). *Higher Education and the Public Good: Imagining the University*. London: Bloomsbury.

OECD (n.d.). *Database – PISA 2012*, OECD. Retrieved from http://pisa2012.acer.edu.au/interactive.php (accessed 12 May 2014).

OECD (2010). PISA 2009 Results: What Makes a School Successful? – Resources, Policies and Practices (Volume IV) http://dx.doi.org/10.1787/9789264091559-en (accessed 12 April 2017).

OECD (2011a). *Divided We Stand: Why Inequality Keeps Rising*, OECD, Retrieved from http://dx.doi.org/10.1787/9789264119536-en (accessed 25 March 2014.).

OECD (2011b). PISA in Focus N°9: School Autonomy and Accountability: Are They Related to Student Performance? Retrieved from http://www.oecd.org/pisa/48910490.pdf (accessed 15 July 2013).

OECD (2012). 'Public and Private Schools: How Management and Funding Relate to their Socio-economic Profile', OECD. http://dx.doi.org/10.1787/9789264175006-en (accessed 15 July 2013).

Ofsted (n.d.) Ofsted | Sands School. Retrieved from https://reports.ofsted.gov.uk/provider/27/113619 (accessed 20 January 2020).

Olssen, M., Codd, J. and O'Neill, A.-M. (2004). *Education Policy: Globalization, Citizenship and Democracy*. London: Sage.

Olssen, M., and Peters, M. A. (2005). 'Neoliberalism, Higher Education and the Knowledge Economy: From the Free Market to Knowledge Capitalism'. *Journal of Education Policy*, 20(3): 313–45. doi:10.1080/02680930500108718.

Owen-Smith, J. (2018). *Research Universities and the Public Good: Discovery for an Uncertain Future*. Redwood City: Stanford University Press.

Ozga, J. (1987). 'Studying Education Policy through the Lives of Policy Makers'. In S. Walker and L. Barton (eds), *Changing Policies, Changing Teachers: New Directions for Schooling?* Philadelphia, PA: Open University Press, pp. 138–50.

Parish N., Baxter, A. and Sandals, L. (2012). *Action Research into the Evolving Role of the Local Authority In Education, the Final Report for the Ministerial Advisory Group, DfE* (Research Report DFE – RR224). London: DfE.

Patmore, G., and Balnave, N. (2018). *A Global History of Co-operative Business*. Abingdon: Routledge.

Peters, M., and Marshall, J. (1996). *Individualism and Community: Education and Social Policy in the Postmodern Condition*. London: Falmer Press.

Powell, W. W., and Rerup, C. (2017). 'Opening the Black Box: The Microfoundations of Institutions'. In R. Greenwood, C. Oliver, T. B. Lawrence and R. E. Meyer (eds), *The Sage Handbook of Organizational Institutionalism* (2nd edn) 311–37. Thousand Oaks, CA: Sage.

Public Administration Select Committee (PASC) (2013). *The Role of the Charity Commission and "Public Benefit": Postlegislative Scrutiny of the Charities Act 2006*. London: The Stationery Office Limited.

Ramirez, F., and Boli, J. (1987). 'The Political Construction of Mass Schooling: European Origins and Worldwide Institutionalization'. *Sociology of Education*, 60(1): 2–17.

Rawolle, S., Rowlands, J. and Blackmore, J. (2017). 'The Implications of Contractualism for the Responsibilisation of Higher Education'. *Discourse: Studies in the Cultural Politics of Education*, 38(1): 109–22. doi:10.1080/01596306.2015.1104856.

Readhead, Z. (2009). FAQ QAs-2009. 10pp. Retrieved from http://www.summerhillschool.co.uk/pages/themeeting.html (accessed 10 July 2013).

Reay, D. (2012). *What Would a Socially Just Education System Look Like?* London: The Centre for Labour and Social Studies.

Reeves, A., and Loopstra, R. (2017). '"Set Up to Fail"? How Welfare Conditionality Undermines Citizenship for Vulnerable Groups'. *Social Policy and Society*, 16(2): 327–38. doi:10.1017/S1474746416000646.

Resnick, P. (1997). *Twenty-First Century Democracy*. Montreal: McGill-Queen's University Press.

Robertson, S., and Dale, R. (2013). 'The Social Justice Implications of Privatisation in Education Governance Frameworks: A Relational Account'. *Oxford Review of Education*, 39(4): 426–45.

Robertson, S., Mundy, K., Verger, A. and Menashy, F. (eds) (2012). *Public Private Partnerships in Education: New Actors and Modes of Governance in a Globalizing World.* Cheltenham: Edward Elgar.

Robertson, S., Mundy, K., Verger, A. and Menashy, F. (2012). 'An introduction to public private partnerships and education governance'. In S. Robertson, K. Mundy, A. Verger and F. Menashy (eds), *Public Private Partnerships in Education: New Actors and Modes of Governance in a Globalizing World.* Cheltenham: Edward Elgar, pp. 1–17.

Rogers (2010). 'Academy Schools: Full List of Those Who Have Registered an Interest'. *The Guardian.* Retrieved from http://www.guardian.co.uk/news/datablog/2010/jul/19/academy-schools-list-applied (accessed 15 May 2012).

Rugby School (2014). Public Benefit. Retrieved from https://www.rugbyschool.co.uk/about/governance/public-benefit/ (accessed 5 July 2019).

Ryan, C., and Sibieta, L. (2010) *Private Schooling in the UK and Australia*, Institute for Fiscal Studies. Retrieved from http://www.ifs.org.uk/bns/bn106.pdf (accessed 8 March 2011).

Sahlberg, P. (2014). *Finnish Lessons 2. 0.* New York: Teachers College Press.

Sanderson, I. (2009). 'Intelligent Policy Making for a Complex World: Pragmatism, Evidence and Learning'. *Political Studies,* 57(4): 699–719.

Sands School (2010). Sands School. Retrieved from http://www.sands-school.co.uk/ (accessed 19 October 2010).

Scottish Government (2017). *Scottish Budget: Draft Budget 2018–2019.* Edinburgh, Scotland: The Scottish Government.

Singh, P., Thomas, S. and Harris, J. (2013) 'Recontextualising Policy Discourses: A Bernsteinian Perspective on Policy Interpretation, Translation, Enactment'. *Journal of Education Policy,* 28(4): 465–480. doi:10.1080/02680939.2013.770554.

Singh, P. (2014). Totally Pedagogised Society: Contributions to Critical Policy Studies. Educationalization, Pedagogisation and Globalisation. presented at the meeting of the 8th International Basil Bernstein Symposium, Nanzan University's Nagoya Campus, Nagoya, Japan. Retrieved from https://research-repository.griffith.edu.au/bitstream/handle/10072/64025/98307_1.pdf (accessed 20 January 2020).

Simkins, T. (1997). 'Autonomy and Accountability'. In B. Fidler, S. Russell and T. Simkins (eds), *Choices for Self-Managing Schools: Autonomy and Accountability.* London: BELMAS.

Simkins, T. (1999). 'Values, Power and Instrumentality: Theory and Research in Education Management'. *Educational Management and Administration,* 27 (3): 267–81.

Spring, J. (2008). 'Research on Globalization and Education'. *Review of Educational Research,* 78(2): 330–63. doi:10.3102/0034654308317846.

Stabe and Jones (22 March 2011). Council Cuts: UK LAs Respond to Budget Cuts, *Financial Times.* Retrieved from http://www.ft.com/cms/s/0/f11f1a48-40d3-11e0-9a37-00144feabdc0.html (accessed 15 May 2012).

Stanford (2018). University Code of Conduct. Retrieved from https://adminguide.stanford.edu/chapter-1/subchapter-1/policy-1-1-1 (accessed 22 July 2019).

Starr, P. (1988). 'The Meaning of Privatization'. *Yale Law and Policy Review*, 6: 6–41.

Sutton Trust & Social Mobility Commission (2019). *Elitist Britain 2019: The Educational Backgrounds of Britain's Leading People*. Sutton Trust & Crown.

Tamboukou, M. (2012). 'History and Ethnography: Interfaces and Juxtapositions'. In S. Delamont (ed.), *Handbook of Qualitative Research in Education*. Cheltenham: Elgar, pp. 82–91.

Thompson, G., Savage, G. and Lingard, B. (2016). 'Introduction'. *The Australian Educational Researcher*, 43(1): 1–13.

Tomorrow's Schools Independent Taskforce (2018). *Our Schooling Futures: Stronger Together: Whiria Ngā Kura Tūātinitini: Report by the Tomorrow's Schools Independent Taskforce*. Wellington: Ministry of Education.

Trimmer, K. (2013). 'Independent Public Schools: A Move to Increased Autonomy and Devolution of Decision-making in Western Australian Public Schools'. *Childhood Education*, 89(3): 178–84. doi:10.1080/00094056.2013.792703.

Truss, E. (2013, March 18). Elizabeth Truss Speaks on the National Curriculum to the Fellowship Commission: Speech. Retrieved from https://www.gov.uk/government/speeches/elizabeth-truss-speaks-on-the-national-curriculum-to-the-fellowship-commission (accessed 13 August 2013).

UNESCO (2002). *Global Monitoring Report: Education for All*. Paris, France: UNESCO.

UNESCO (2016). Education 2030: Incheon Declaration and Framework for Action for the Implementation of Sustainable Development Goal 4 (available at http://en.unesco.org/education2030-sdg4, accessed 22 July 2019).

UNICEF UK & Refugee Support Network (2018). Education for Refugee and Asylum Seeking Children: Access and Equality in England, Scotland and Wales. www.unicef.org.uk/wp-content/uploads/2018/09/Access-to-Education-report-PDF.pdf (accessed 30 August 2019).

Verger, A., Fontdevila, C. and Parcerisa, L. (2019). 'Reforming Governance through Policy Instruments: How and to What Extent Standards, Tests and Accountability in Education Spread Worldwide'. *Discourse: Studies in the Cultural Politics of Education*, 40(2): 248–70. doi:10.1080/01596306.2019.1569882.

Waks, L. J. (2010). 'Dewey's Theory of the Democratic Public and the Public Character of Charter Schools'. *Educational Theory*, 60(6): 665–81. doi:10.1111/j.1741-5446.2010.00383.x.

Waks, L. J. (2017). 'Introduction to Part I'. In A. R. English and L. J. Waks (eds), *John Dewey's Democracy and Education: A Centennial Handbook*. Cambridge: Cambridge University Press, pp. 5–14.

Wahlström, N. (2010). 'A European Space for Education Looking for Its Public', *European Educational Research Journal*, 9(4): 432–43.

Warner, M. (2002). 'Publics and Counterpublics'. *Public Culture*, 14(1): 49–90.

Webster, A., Brown, A., Stewart, D., Walton, J. K. and Shaw, L. (eds) (2012). *The Hidden Alternative: Co-operative Values, Past, Present and Future*, Tokyo: United Nations University Press.

Wells, A. S., Slayton, J. and Scott, J. (2002). 'Defining Democracy in the Neoliberal Age: Charter School Reform and Educational Consumption'. *American Educational Research Journal*, 39(2): 337–61. doi:10.3102/00028312039002337.

West, A., and Bailey, E. (2013). 'The Development of the Academies Programme: "Privatising" School-Based Education in England 1986–2013'. *British Journal of Educational Studies*, 61(2): 137–59.

West, A., Barham, E., and Hind, A. (2011). 'Secondary School Admissions in England 2001 to 2008: Changing Legislation, Policy and Practice'. *Oxford Review of Education*, 37(1), 1–20. doi:10.1080/03054985.2010.538527.

Wilson, T. S. (2011). 'Civic Fragmentation or Voluntary Association? Habermas, Fraser, and Charter School Segregation'. *Educational Theory*, 60(6): 643–64. doi:10.1111/j.1741-5446.2010.00382.x.

Woodin, T. (2014). 'Co-Operative Schools: Putting Values into Practice'. In T. Woodin (ed.), *Co-operation, Learning and Co-operative Values: Contemporary Issues in Education*. London: Taylor and Francis: ProQuest Ebook Central.

Wilson, T. (2010). 'Civic Fragmentation or Voluntary Association? Habermas, Fraser, and Charter School Segregation'. *Educational Theory*, 60 (6): 643–64.

Wilson, T. S. (2012). 'Negotiating Public and Private: Philosophical Frameworks for School Choice'. In G. Miron, K. Welner, P. Hinchley and W. Mathis (eds), *Exploring the School Choice Universe: Evidence And Recommendations*. Information Age Press, 2012. http://ebookcentral.proquest.com/lib/aut/detail.action?docID=1826765.

Wylie, C. (2009). 'Tomorrow's Schools after 20 Years: Can a System of Self-Managing Schools Live Up to Its Initial Aims?'. *The New Zealand Annual Review of Education* (19). doi:10.26686/nzaroe.v0i19.1555.

Yeatman, A. (1996). 'Interpreting Contemporary Contractualism'. *Australian Journal of Social Issues*, 31(1): 39–54.

Yeatman, A. (2007). 'Varieties of Individualism'. In C. Howard (ed.), *Contested Individualization: Debates about Contemporary Personhood*. New York: Palgrave Macmillan, pp. 45–59.

Yeatman, A. (2015). 'Freedom and the Question of Institutional Design'. In A. Yeatman (ed.), *Neoliberalism and the Crisis of Public Institutions Working Papers in the Human Rights and Public Life Program*. Sydney: The Whitlam Institute within Western Sydney University, pp. 19–35.

Zimmer, R., Gill, B., Booker, K., Lavertud, S. and Witte, J. (2012) 'Examining Charter Student Achievement Effects across Seven States'. *Economics of Education Review* 31: 213–24.

Index

academy schools, England 37–41, 45, 61–4
 democratic co-option 31
 conversion 151–4
 curriculum 50
 demographics 45, 63, 136
 governance 37, 39, 144
 leaders 36
 services 144–5
 trusts 40, 45, 59, 62, 92
authoritarian control 16, 109–10

Bernstein, Basil 12–14, 114–15, 118–20, 122–4, 126, 130
boundaries, legitimacy of 33–4, 67, 69, 83, 109–10, 149
brokerage 21, 40, 145
Building Schools for the Future 79–80

capital 21, 48, 55, 81, 126
 cultural 54, 55
 economic 48, 78–9
 human capital 9, 79, 91, 135–6
capitalism 28, 111, 113
Charitable Incorporated Organization 77, 95
charities 17, 50–3, 76
 public benefit and 52, 94–5
 schools 51, 62, 87–8, 94–5, 106
 universities 86
charter schools 37, 38, 40, 61–2, 113–14
citizenship 1, 19, 33, 69, 91, 110
class analysis 54, 104, 114–15, 122–4
codes of conduct and ethics 86–7
Community Benefit Societies 74, 76
company law 50–1, 72, 81
complex society 31, 36
compulsory schooling 53–4, 58, 61
conditionally public 7, 18, 29–30, 42, 43, 83–4
 accountability 129–31
 counterpublics 153, 159
 entities 68–72

private schools 53–6
consultancy 18, 59, 68
consumerism 29, 42, 129
co-operative schools 65–67, 71, 75
co-operatives and mutuals 65–7, 70–1, 73–5, 81, 95, 143
corporations 73
 community interest 61, 81, 95, 143
 public benefit 75–6, 85–6
counterpublic 8, 20, 29, 38, 88
 Sands School as 115, 129–31, 153
crown entities 75, 158

decision-making 16–17, 24–5, 33, 41, 69
 publics 8, 19, 29–32, 130
 responsibilization and 111
 school 103, 116–17, 131
 stewardship and 81, 158
democracy 16–17, 24, 30–2, 36–7, 68–70, 149
 all-affected principle 33
 all-subjected principle 33–4, 69
 education and 16, 23–4, 27, 124
 publics and 156
 religion and 93
 state and 2, 6, 25, 28
democratic equality 47–8, 91, 95–6, 106–7
democratic ideal 27, 75, 96, 105
democratic participation 7, 124
democratic schooling 1–2, 31, 38–9, 97, 113, 115
demos 36, 156
deprivation 59, 63, 116, 151–2
Dewey, John 16–17, 23–42, 44, 89–92, 104, 123–4
direct subsidy scheme schools 35, 62
Durkheim, David Émile 36, 112–14

economy, the 28–30, 129
elite education 7, 54–56, 92–4, 104, 122, 127
emergence 155–6

equality legislation 77, 94
equality of access 2, 35, 54, 56–9, 110, 135
exempt status 17, 76–7, 86
experts 27, 32, 36, 91–2
extended case method 15, 100

for-profit 50–1, 75–6, 81–2, 86–7, 100–102
framing and classification 13, 114, 118–22, 130–1
free schools 37, 112–13
Fraser, Nancy 17, 22, 123
    publics and 7–8, 28–30, 105, 107
    transnationalism and 33
    social justice and 33–4, 41, 69

governance 8, 102
    democratic 1, 89, 129
    hierarchical and market, 13
    private interests in 18, 50–1, 61–2, 88, 102
    school 10–11, 37–8, 45, 102–4, 150–3, 157–9
    self- 19, 29–30, 110
    structures 33–4, 44, 65–84, 105–7
government funding 27, 40, 59, 66, 79, 133–6
globalization 9, 15, 17, 32–3, 37
greater community 17, 32–3, 36–7

Habermas, Jürgen 8, 22, 28–30, 42, 129, 156
Headmasters and Headmistresses Conference 54–5
higher education 56, 82, 86–7, 104

Independent Public Schools 8, 35, 45, 62
Independent School Standards 5, 20, 50, 87, 93
Independent Schools Council (ISC) 51, 87–8, 94, 100
individualism 14, 19–21, 24–7, 112–13, 130, 158
    autonomous 25
    collectivist 109, 149
    competitive 43, 87, 134
    co-operative 113
individualization 20, 25, 39, 111–12, 130, 139–40
industrialization 32, 42, 73, 111

innovation 48–9, 61
    curriculum 117–19, 128, 131
    governance and 18, 61
    public services and 21, 138, 141–3, 150
    school 10, 53, 94, 113–14
institutional isomorphism 49–50
international democratic education network 116
invisible pedagogy 114–15, 119, 122–3

liability 72–4
local authorities in England 66, 78–9, 133–48, 150–1
    privatization and 21, 39, 59–61, 72–3
    services *see* public service and services to schools
    statutory responsibilities 63, 144–5, 147
local government 44, 60, 104, 139, 150
Locke, John 53–4

Māori schooling 10, 158
    kura hourua 40
market, the 22, 65, 67–70, 106–7
    choice and 25–6
    educational services and 21, 40, 59–60, 138–9, 144–8
    governance 13, 18, 71
    public and 5, 9, 11, 30
    risk and 19, 80
    schooling and 21, 39, 55–6, 105, 123, 126–30
    state and 110–11
middle classes 54, 114, 122, 129
modernization 32, 107

neoliberal reform 10, 16, 24, 64, 78–80, 110
neoliberalism 9, 35–6, 110–11
    individual and 21, 130
    state and 20, 22, 28, 39, 83
new contractualism 25, 139–40, 147
Nolan Committee principles of public life 86–7
not-for-profit 62, 75–6, 80–1, 85–7, 102

OECD 9, 33, 38, 62–4, 92
open schooling 114–15
opinion formation 19, 30–1, 69, 155

organic and mechanical solidarity 113–14
organizational convergence 49, 51
organizational relationships 49, 78

partnership schools 40–1
personalism, critique of 26–7
PISA *see* OECD
policy 6, 64
   choice and 24–6, 37
   history 54
   privatization and 18, 35, 59, 110, 134
   public good and 47, 57, 157–8
   study of 5, 12–14
   transnational 8, 17, 32–3, 63
political authority 31, 33, 130–1
popular opinion 26–7, 158
private education 5, 17, 43, 45–8,
   53–6, 159
   girls' 54
Private Finance Initiatives 78–80
private good 47–8, 56–7, 61, 91
private ownership 18, 58
private schools 18–20, 48, 50–6,
   89–90, 92–6
   charitable status 76–8, 87–8
   co-operative 74–5
   counterpublic 129–30, 153
   democratic 1–2, 6–7, 126–7
   elite 'public' 7, 54–5, 122
   equality and 105–7
   research on 96–9
   social inequality and 91
   state funding and 45, 62
private sector 5, 17, 30, 48–9, 78–9, 89
   innovation and 94, 106
   local authorities and 146
privatization 2, 5, 110
   education 18
   endogenous/exogenous 57–8
   public interests and 70, 83, 150
   public services and 21, 59–60,
   133–5, 147–8
   schooling 37, 61–3, 113–14
   scrutiny of 25, 30
public accountability 20–1, 26, 95, 109,
   120, 129–31
public benefit 17–19, 51–3, 75–8, 83,
   85–8, 94–5
public choice theory 9, 24–5

public education 2–3, 5–9, 16–17, 26–7,
   69–70, 149–50
   counterpublic 22
   pluralist 149
   schooling 2, 34–5, 53–4, 67, 109–10
   specialization in 41–2
public good 19–20, 47, 56–7, 86–8,
   90–1, 106–7
public opinion 8, 26–7, 28, 31–2, 33
public service 21, 25, 60, 78,
   133–5, 139–44
public sphere 7–8, 22, 27–31, 153
   bourgeoisie 18, 22, 28
public–private partnerships (PPP) 19,
   47, 78–80
publics 7–8, 22, 27–30, 31, 42, 154–6
   actual 17, 20, 26, 97, 107, 150
   bounded 33, 69, 75, 83, 110, 133
   emergent 19, 36, 83, 109, 155
   ideal 6, 156
   limits to 55, 68
   localized 16, 29–30, 32, 36, 105, 152–4
   normative 156
   pluralist 36–7, 39–40, 41, 105,
   109, 129–31
   transnational 17, 29, 33–4, 105
   unbounded 34, 36, 68–70, 83,
   149–50, 155–6

reciprocal constitution 25, 44–5, 49, 109,
   112–13, 153
recontextualization 11–13, 70, 150–4
reflexive science 14–15, 41
responsibilization 20, 41, 87, 111
risk 53, 78–80, 83, 84, 111–12, 145–8

school autonomy 8, 31, 37–8, 61–4,
   150–4, 156–8
schooling 2, 23, 30–1, 34–7, 53–6, 61–4
   attainment and qualifications 59, 91, 99,
   110, 114, 151
   admissions 35, 59, 76–7, 158
   assessment 37, 63–4
   curriculum 50, 67, 91, 114–15,
   117–21, 127–9
   governance *see* governance
   inspection 10–11, 37, 50, 152
school choice 24–6, 37. *See also* public
   choice theory

service learning 91, 98
service user 25–6, 74
services to schools 21, 59–61, 133, 136, 146–8
  corporate model of 72–3, 139–40, 144–5
  co-operative model of 65–6, 73, 143–4, 150
  community engagement model of 140–1
  entrepreneurial model of 141–3
  social enterprise and 81
  statutory or traded 63, 72, 134–5, 145–6
social cohesion 36, 80, 111, 112–13
social efficiency 47, 90–1
social enterprise 80–2
social fields 49, 55, 114, 122–3, 126–7
  agency 49, 135, 155
  structuration 49
social justice 33–4, 38, 39–41, 43, 47, 112–13
  feminist 29
social mobility 47, 90–1, 92–93, 106–7
social reproduction 122–3
solidarity. *See* organic and mechanical solidarity
sovereignty 20, 29, 112, 130, 154
standardization 37, 38–9, 41–2
state, the 5–6, 27–8, 39
  authority 29, 34, 69, 109–10
  authoritarian 12–13, 16, 110–11
  centralism 110
  economy and 123, 130
  entrepreneurial 48–9, 141
  nation 8, 36
  officials of 31, 32
  schooling 129, 153
  subjection 33–4, 68–9

Tomorrow's Schools 9–10, 157–9
totally pedagogized society 13, 123

United Nations 32–3, 35, 58

Yeatman, Anna 20–1, 25, 111–12

Lightning Source UK Ltd.
Milton Keynes UK
UKHW052228130720
366477UK00003B/148